Date Due

*Ethical
Standards
of the
Accounting
Profession*

Ethical Standards of the Accounting Profession

JOHN L. CAREY AND WILLIAM O. DOHERTY

American Institute of Certified Public Accountants

Disclaimer

In publishing this book, the American Institute of Certified Public Accountants accepts no responsibility for what is said. The book has not been reviewed or approved by any committee of the Institute. The fact that its authors are members of the Institute's staff does not give the book any standing as an official statement of the Institute.

The opinions expressed are those of the authors alone, and responsibility for factual accuracy rests entirely upon them.

PREFACE

To call this book a revision of John L. Carey's *Professional Ethics of Certified Public Accountants,* published in 1956, is an understatement requiring some explanation. It is true that the current version, like its predecessor, has three main parts and eleven chapters. A glance at the table of contents will reveal that many of the same subjects are again being dealt with, and in substantially the same order. In short, the plan of the older book has been retained—a plan which emphasizes general ethical principles as guides to practitioners in determining the proper course to follow in specific circumstances.

But the details of the earlier book have been altered drastically. This has been necessitated in part by the many changes that have been effected in the profession's rules in the past decade. The Institute's Code now has twenty-one rules compared to the sixteen it had in 1956. In addition, many of the older rules have been revised to meet the changing conditions of professional practice. In general, the state CPA societies and the state boards of accountancy have made corresponding changes in their codes, with the result that the various ethical rules under which CPAs practice are more nearly uniform now than ever before.

Another factor that has occasioned this detailed revision of the 1956 book is the issuance by the Institute's ethics committee of interpretive opinions. Those which are of general application are published in *The CPA* and are then given permanent form as an appendix to the Code of Professional Ethics. The seventeen opinions which have been issued up to now are reprinted in Appendix C of this book. They are referred to throughout the book and have exerted an important influence on many of the views expressed. Other interpretive opinions deal with specific ethics questions raised by practitioners. These frequently appear in *The CPA* in the form of summarized questions and answers. Many of the more significant rulings in this category appear in Appendix D.

It would be tedious to recite in detail the precise effect of this refining of the profession's standards on the text of this book. But an illustration of the method of revision might be of interest. The Independence chapter of *Professional Ethics of Certified Public Accountants* was written when there was no rule on independence. In fact, the word itself did not even appear in the Code. The only explicit guidance on the concept was old Rule 13. This was a financial interest rule that was fine as far as it went but it left much unsaid and was often difficult to apply. Whatever additional precepts there were had to be inferred from the rules dealing with reporting standards, contingent fees, commissions and fee sharing, and incompatible occupations. Also additional general information on independence could be obtained from the professional literature, from releases of the Securities and Exchange Commission, and from official statements of professional societies. This state of affairs necessitated a treatment of independence as a concept that was at best general and at worst vague. But all this was changed by the adoption of the current Rule 1.01

in 1962. This established reasonably clear-cut standards of independence in the principal areas of difficulty and suggested broader criteria for other areas. Stimulated no doubt by discussion over the adoption of the new rule, CPAs began to write and speak about independence in more specific terms. They challenged many of the traditional views on the subject. Their challenges evoked responses and closer examination of the questions involved. Additional interpretive rulings of the committee were then issued. Naturally all of these developments had a profound influence on the presentation of the topic in Chapter 3 of this book. The result has been a complete transformation of the chapter.

Other chapters have been similarly affected. Chapter 4 ("The Professional Attitude") has been adjusted to take into account the changes in the rules on advertising, solicitation, and commissions and fee-sharing, as well as the changes in the formal opinions interpreting these rules. Chapter 5 ("Opinions on Financial Statements") has been completely revised because of the adoption of new rules, the issuance of new statements on auditing standards and procedures, and the promulgation of Opinions of the Accounting Principles Board. Chapter 6 ("Tax Practice") has been thoroughly rewritten to give effect to the new literature, particularly the Statements on Responsibilities in Tax Practice by the Institute's committee on Federal taxation. Chapter 7 ("Ethical Responsibilities in Management Services") reflects the new developments in this field, especially the impact on accounting ethics of the computer revolution.

All of these changes—including less significant ones in all the other chapters—seemed to justify a new title for the book in order to emphasize the fact that it is not simply an editorial revision of the older work.

The following members of the Institute have read chapters in manuscript and have generously given us the benefit of their advice and experience: Andrew Barr, Herman Bevis, Thomas Flynn, Ira N. Frisbee, Thomas Graves, Louis H.

Penney, and Robert M. Trueblood. We are grateful also to the following members of the Institute's staff who have reviewed parts of the manuscript and offered suggestions for improvement: Henry DeVos, John Lawler, Richard Lytle, Beatrice Melcher, Richard Nest, Charles Noyes, Roderic A. Parnell, Gilbert Simonetti and Reed Storey.

Other members of the staff who assembled material, typed the manuscript, and produced the book are: Donald J. Schneeman, William H. Van Rensselaer, Norma Lazarus, Catherine J. Wilheim, James D. Bennett, Joan Lucas, and Ann O'Rourke.

Our indebtedness to others is more difficult to acknowledge because it is so pervasive. We have reviewed the rather large—and, happily, growing—literature on the profession's ethics and have found it an invaluable aid. Over the years we have talked with hundreds of certified public accountants about questions of accounting ethics. Particularly helpful in clarifying concepts have been members of the Institute's committee on professional ethics, present and past. But perhaps our greatest debt is to those thousands of practitioners who have had to decide on a proper course of conduct and have written the Institute for guidance. From them we acquired more knowledge about our subject than would otherwise have been possible.

JOHN L. CAREY
WILLIAM O. DOHERTY

New York, N.Y., January 1966

Contents

PART ONE

General Principles of Ethics

Chapter 1

PROFESSIONAL ETHICS AND
THE PUBLIC INTEREST

PROFESSIONAL ethics forms a small part of a complex system of discipline which civilized society has imposed on itself through laws, customs, moral standards, social etiquette—rules of many kinds, enforced in many ways. If people are to live together in peace, discipline is necessary to restrain the predatory instincts with which man is born.

The assurance that such discipline exists is the basis of man's faith in his fellow man, which, despite frequent disappointments, is essential to sustain the complex economic structure which now supports most of the population of the free world.

Sec. 1 — PURPOSES OF PROFESSIONAL ETHICS

A code of professional ethics is a voluntary assumption of self-discipline above and beyond the requirements of the law. It serves the highly practical purpose of notifying the public that the profession will protect the public interest. The

3

code in effect is an announcement that, in return for the faith which the public reposes in them, members of the profession accept the obligation to behave in a way that will be beneficial to the public.

The ethical code also provides members of the profession with guides to the type of behavior which the historical experience of the profession as a whole has indicated is most likely to attract the confidence of the public.

A code of ethics is therefore a practical working tool. It is as necessary to a professional practitioner as his theoretical principles and technical procedures. Without a system of professional ethics he would be incomplete.

When people need a doctor, or a lawyer, or a certified public accountant, they seek someone whom they can trust to do a good job—not for himself, but for them. They have to trust him, since they cannot appraise the quality of his service. They must take it on faith that he is competent, and that his primary motive is to help them.

That is why professions are distinguished from businesses and why professional men enjoy special prestige.

Professional men and women are accepted as persons highly skilled in some science or art, who desire to serve the public, and who place service ahead of personal gain. If they were not regarded in this light they would have no patients or clients. Who would engage a doctor, or a lawyer, or a certified public accountant who was known to put personal rewards ahead of service to his patient or client? How could anyone know whether to take his advice or not? If the practitioner were mainly interested in making money, he might be tempted to keep his patients sick, or keep his client in litigation, or extend his audit beyond the necessary scope. Who would engage such a man?

Not only must people believe that the professional man will not take advantage of them financially, but also that they can safely entrust him with their most private and vital affairs. He must be regarded as a man of character. He must act in a way that strengthens their confidence. He must display a professional attitude toward his work.

A professional attitude must be learned. It is not a natural gift. It is natural to be selfish—to place personal gain ahead of service. That is precisely why the people as a whole honor the relatively few—professional men and other true public servants —who have disciplined themselves to follow the harder course.

The rules of ethics, therefore, are the foundation of public confidence.

Public confidence may be even more important to a certified public accountant than to other professional men. The CPA must have not only the confidence of those who become his clients, but also the confidence of those who rely on his reports. His service may be of little value to a client if a bank, for example, will not have faith in his report. And the bank, or the credit agency, or the government agency, or other "third parties" who may rely on the report, will have faith in it only if they believe that the CPA has a responsibility to look out for their interests, as well as the client's.

Since all the countless third parties who may rely on the reports of certified public accountants cannot know the CPAs personally, it is essential that they must have confidence in CPAs generally—as a group which can be trusted by all concerned.

Sec. 2 — IDEALS, ETHICS AND RULES OF CONDUCT

The word "ethics" in general usage means the philosophy of human conduct with emphasis on "right" and "wrong," which are moral questions.

"Professional ethics," however, does not involve moral questions exclusively. There is nothing immoral, for example, in truthful advertising, but it is unethical for physicians, lawyers and certified public accountants to advertise their professional services, no matter how truthfully.

Actually the professions have borrowed the word "ethics" from general usage and have applied it in the narrowed sense of the basic principles of right action for members of the profession concerned.

"Right action" for a professional man will of course include conformity with moral standards, but will also include behavior designed for practical as well as idealistic purposes.

"Ideals" are standards conceived as perfect, not yet attained, perhaps even unattainable. Ideals are goals. They are not enforceable by rules.

A code of professional ethics may be designed in part to encourage ideal behavior, but basically such a code is intended to be enforceable. It should be at a higher level than the law, but it must be at a lower level than the ideal. It is a practical working tool.

"Professional ethics," therefore, may be regarded as a mixture of moral and practical concepts, with a sprinkling of exhortation to ideal conduct designed to evoke "right action" on the part of members of the profession concerned—all reduced to rules which are intended to be enforceable, to some extent at least, by disciplinary action.

Sec. 3 — ORIGIN OF RULES OF ETHICS FOR CPAS

Where do the ethical rules for CPAs originate? In the American Institute of Certified Public Accountants; in state societies of certified public accountants; and in boards of accountancy in forty jurisdictions where such rules have been promulgated under authority of law. While not identical, the rules of these various bodies are similar. The basic principles are the same, though the form, arrangement and extent of coverage may differ. The rules of the Institute govern the professional conduct of the largest number of certified public accountants, and these rules are most widely known outside the profession. They have been adopted in whole or in part by many of the state societies. Consequently, in this book, the Institute's rules will be the principal basis of discussion.

Sec. 4 — EVOLUTION OF RULES

These rules have developed by evolutionary processes over a period of sixty years or more. They did not spring full-blown from the mind of any individual. They are the product of thousands of minds, guided by the experience of decades. Many of them were adopted as the result of specific events which disclosed the need for additional standards. Many important ethical questions are not yet covered in the official rules, and new questions are constantly arising.

Growth and change are therefore characteristic of rules of professional conduct. As the practice of accounting becomes more widespread, more varied and more complex, ethical questions arise which had not arisen before. Patterns of ethical concepts change as a profession develops. Existing rules have often been modified or elaborated. The ethical codes of the medical and legal professions have developed in the same way.

Ethical concepts are not fixed, final or precise. They reflect the experience of a group, and the sense of responsibility which it has developed up to a given point in time.

Sec. 5 — ENFORCEMENT OF RULES

Professional Societies. The Institute's Code of Professional Ethics derives its authority from the by-laws of the Institute, which provide that the Trial Board may admonish, suspend, or expel a member who is found guilty, after a hearing, of infringing any of the by-laws or any provision of the Code of

Professional Ethics. Publication of the respondent's name in the official statement of the case is discretionary with the Trial Board. It should be emphasized that any act held to be discreditable to the profession may be grounds for discipline, and a member is under obligation to exercise his judgment and his conscience in doubtful areas. In fact, the preamble to the Code states that the enumeration of the rules "should not be construed as a denial of the existence of other standards of conduct not specifically mentioned."*

The state societies of certified public accountants enforce their rules generally as the Institute does. Expulsion, suspension, or admonition are the penalties for violations.

Effectiveness of Societies' Rules. Critics have pointed out that a CPA may be expelled from a professional society, but continue in practice in defiance of its rules. However, experience shows that there is a strong restraining force in the possible humiliation of disciplinary proceedings and impairment of professional reputation. The deterrent effect of the rules of the professional societies has been demonstrated to be very powerful.

State Laws. But what about certified public accountants who do not become members of any professional society? In forty jurisdictions boards of accountancy, under authority of law, have promulgated rules of professional conduct. In these states a CPA's certificate may be suspended or revoked for violation of the rules. This is, of course, an even stronger deterrent than the possibility of expulsion from a society.

Legally enforceable rules of conduct exist in thirty jurisdictions having so-called "regulatory" laws, in which neither a certified public accountant nor a public accountant may practice without a license. In these states ethical violations may result in loss of the license to practice—the most effective deterrent of all.

*See below, page 183.

All accountancy laws provide for suspension or revocation of CPA certificates and licenses to practice, where such licenses exist, for felony, fraud, false or misleading statements, and similar gross offenses.

Since the populous states of California, New York, Pennsylvania, Ohio, Texas, Michigan, New Jersey, Florida and Massachusetts, in addition to thirty-one others, now have legally enforceable rules of conduct, it is clear that by far the greater part of the country's CPA population is subject to such rules. It may be hoped that before long this will be true in all states.

Internal Revenue Service. A CPA who is entitled to practice before the Internal Revenue Service may be disbarred or suspended for failure to conduct his practice "in accordance with recognized ethical standards,"* as well as for violation of specific rules of conduct to which the Internal Revenue Service requires those who represent others before it to conform.

Securities and Exchange Commission. The Securities and Exchange Commission may also take disciplinary action against CPAs who do not possess the "requisite qualifications to represent others" or who are "lacking in character or integrity" or who "have engaged in unethical or improper professional conduct."** In addition, the Commission will not accept financial statements containing opinions of certified public accountants or public accountants who are not "independent" as provided in its rules.† Independence is an important ethical concept in professional accounting.

Institute Proposal to Improve Enforcement. The Institute's Council in May 1960, on recommendation of the committee on long-range objectives, resolved that it is an objective of the Institute to coordinate its activities with those of the

---

* Sec. 10.51 of *Treasury Department Circular No. 230.*
**Rule II (e), Rules of Practice, Securities and Exchange Commission.
† Rule 2-01, Regulation S-X.

state societies and to delineate their respective areas of responsibility, particularly in the direction of adopting a uniform code of ethics and enforcement procedures. Since that time considerable progress has been made towards adopting a uniform code. The question of coordinating enforcement procedures is receiving further study.

Progress in Enforcement. In the last few years great improvements have been made in enforcement machinery at both state and national levels.

The public interest is better protected against abuses of confidence reposed in the accounting profession than the public has yet learned to know.

Chapter 2

PROFESSIONAL COMPETENCE

THE public expects three things from anyone who holds himself out as a qualified member of a recognized profession—competence, responsibility and a desire to serve the public.

Competence, in this context, means mastery of a field of technical subject matter requiring advanced intellectual training. Responsibility means reliability, integrity and independence. Acceptance of the obligation to serve the public is reflected in the professional attitude.

The Institute's Code deals extensively with matters that relate to professional responsibility and the professional attitude. It does not have much to say about the subject of competence in general, although Article 2 does require adherence to standards of accounting, auditing and reporting. The preamble to the Code also states that it is a member's obligation to maintain high standards of technical competence and to strive continuously to improve his professional skills.

11

Sec. 6 — COMPETENCE AN ETHICAL OBLIGATION

It seems a basic ethical obligation that a certified public accountant should not render service which he is not competent to render. The client, not being versed in the technique of accounting, has no way of evaluating the competence of the practitioner. He must depend on the certified public accountant, therefore, to do a workmanlike job or to refer him to someone who can.

In fact, the requirement of competence is established by law. If a man offers specialized service to the public and he does not have the degree of skill commonly possessed by others in the same work, he commits a species of fraud on every man who employs him.*

As a matter of ethics, however, professional practitioners may reasonably be expected to carry this principle beyond the minimum limits of a rule of law.

A certified public accountant may have "the degree of skill *commonly* possessed by others," but this does not mean that he may properly accept an engagement in an area unfamiliar to him, requiring knowledge, experience or skill which he does not possess, even though many other CPAs have competence in the area. This principle becomes more important as the scope of accounting practice steadily widens.

Sec. 7 — APPLYING THE CONCEPT OF COMPETENCE

Of course, a rule of reason must prevail.

Any certified public accountant, who has had the conventional professional education and has passed the Uniform CPA Examination, has a foundation of competence. He builds on this foundation by keeping abreast of current accounting literature and by taking courses provided by his professional soci-

*Cooley, *Torts* (4th ed.), 1932, Vol. 3, page 335.

eties, universities, or other organizations. As he performs successive engagements, he will encounter unfamiliar questions with which he can make himself competent to deal by research, study or consultation with more experienced practitioners. Thus his own competence will continually improve and expand.

But if he should be invited to do a kind of work which is wholly unfamiliar, or if he is confronted by a problem which he fears is beyond his capacity, he should ask himself whether, in the time available, he can equip himself for the particular task by study and consultation, or whether in fact the matter is so far beyond his grasp that he would serve his client better to suggest the engagement of someone better qualified in this field.

Sec. 8 — SPECIALIZATION AND REFERRAL

As the accounting profession grows and the scope of practice broadens in response to the needs of business, specialization will increase. This has been the history of older professions, notably medicine. The general practitioner deals with all the ordinary ailments of his patients. He keeps up with developments in all phases of medicine and surgery. When he diagnoses a malady which he believes requires skill he does not possess, he is likely to suggest consultation with a specialist. He can be confident that the specialist will not replace him as the regular family physician.

While some accounting firms have worked together on engagements in this manner to the complete satisfaction of all concerned, this type of consultation or referral is not yet common among CPAs. Perhaps its infrequency is due to fear that the specialist may replace the general practitioner and thenceforth render the regular, recurring accounting services needed by the client. An attempt was made to meet this fear by the adoption of Rule 5.02, which provides in effect that a member who receives an engagement by referral shall not extend his services beyond the specific engagement without first consulting with the referring member.

Some CPAs maintain that this rule is not strong enough. A specialist who has received a referral and is asked by the client to extend his services beyond the referral engagement may indeed "consult with" the referring member. The latter is not likely to agree to the desired extension of services. But his refusal would not be binding on the specialist. One way to protect the original accountant and at the same time encourage referrals to specialists might be to require the consent of, rather than mere consultation with, the referring member. However, such a requirement would hamper the client's right to select his own accountant. Perhaps problems of this kind may be resolved more effectively by agreements between firms than by increased restrictions in the rules.

Sec. 9 — "GROUP COMPETENCE" OF FIRMS

Competence may be attributed to accounting firms (partnerships) as well as to individuals. It is common for partners of a firm to specialize in different kinds of work: for example, in auditing, taxes or management services. The firm may properly accept engagements which any of its partners are competent to conduct, applying the idea of consultation and referral within the firm itself.

Sec. 10 — EMPLOYMENT OF SPECIALISTS

Many CPA firms have widened the scope of their competence by employing nonaccountant specialists as members of their staffs. Since partners must assume professional responsibility for all the work done by their employees, however, it is generally assumed that an accounting firm ought not to accept an engagement to be performed by a staff specialist unless at least one of the partners is competent to evaluate the staff member's work and exercise general supervisory control.

This question is of particular interest as it applies to the expanding field of management services. Some accounting firms employ engineers, actuaries, mathematicians, and other specialists to meet the demands of their clients for a growing variety of services. An ethical question might arise if an accounting firm employed a man who was expert in a field with which none of the partners was familiar, and instructed him to render services for which the firm received fees, but which none of the partners was competent to evaluate or supervise.

Sec. 11 — EMPLOYMENT OF LAWYERS

Spokesmen for bar associations have challenged the propriety of employment of lawyers as members of the staffs of accounting firms on the ground that it amounts to the illegal practice of law by such firms. If a lawyer employed by an accounting firm were permitted to hold himself out as a lawyer, or render to clients of the firm services which only lawyers were authorized to render, the firm would in effect be selling legal services and could be charged with unauthorized practice of law.

However, a member of the bar may properly be employed as a member of the staff of an accounting firm if he does not hold himself out as a lawyer or render any services to clients of the firm which his CPA employers are not authorized to render. Lawyers employed on the staffs of accounting firms presumably are practicing accounting and intend to qualify for the CPA certificate. Many men with degrees in engineering, economics, business administration and other disciplines have entered the practice of accounting and become certified public accountants. Possession of a law degree or admission to the bar should not disqualify anyone from entering the accounting profession. But as an employee of a CPA he may not practice law.

The Institute's Rule 4.03 provides that a member in public practice shall not permit an employee to perform for the member's clients services which the member himself is not permitted to perform.

Sec. 12 — PARTNERSHIPS WITH NON-CPA SPECIALISTS

Ethical questions also arise with respect to the admission of non-CPA specialists to a partnership of certified public accountants. Rule 3.04, which deals with fee splitting, effectively prohibits partnerships with persons not regularly engaged in public accounting as their principal occupation. But the present rules do not prevent partnerships of CPAs with non-CPAs who are engaged in public accounting. The question of whether or not the Code should be amended to outlaw "mixed partnerships" has been considered and will no doubt receive further study.*

It should be noted that even where mixed partnerships are permitted under state laws they cannot be held out to the public as "Certified Public Accountants." Similarly, under the Institute's Code such partnerships cannot be held out as "Members of the American Institute of Certified Public Accountants."

Sec. 13 — COMPLIANCE WITH CONCEPT OF COMPETENCE

To sum up, a certified public accountant should not render services which he is not competent to render, and a firm of

---

*For further discussion of "mixed partnerships," see Chapter 7, pages 114-118.

certified public accountants should not render services which its partners are not permitted to render, or services which no partner is competent to supervise and evaluate. Admittedly, a determination of competence must be subjective. All practitioners and all firms must decide what their limitations are. Doubts should be resolved in the best interest of the client and the public.

Competence will naturally increase both in breadth and depth as a natural result of experience and study. A certified public accountant need not refuse an engagement simply because he knows that some other practitioner might do it better, as long as he feels that he can do it with reasonable competence; that is, do a workmanlike job.

An honest concern for the client's best interests will usually suggest when it is desirable to advise consultation or collaboration, or engagement of another practitioner for a special purpose.

Chapter 3

INDEPENDENCE

INDEPENDENCE, in the sense of being self-reliant, not subordinate, is essential to the practice of all professions. No self-respecting professional man—physician, lawyer or certified public accountant—will subordinate his professional judgment to the views of his patient or client. He cannot evade his professional responsibility for the advice, opinions, and recommendations which he offers. If his patients or clients do not like what he says, the practitioner may regret it; but no one would condone his changing his honest opinion in order to avoid giving offense or to secure his fee.

In all phases of his work—auditing, tax practice and management services—the certified public accountant must be independent in this general sense of the word. If he subordinated his judgment to that of clients, government agencies, bankers, or anyone else, he would not be worth his salt.

Why, then, cannot the matter be left at this point? Why is independence still the subject of debate?

Sec. 14 — INDEPENDENCE IN EXPRESSING OPINIONS
ON FINANCIAL STATEMENTS

The debate continues because independence has come to have a special meaning to certified public accountants in conjunction with audits resulting in opinions on financial statements. Investors, credit grantors, prospective purchasers of businesses, regulatory agencies of government, and others may rely on a CPA's opinion that financial statements fairly reflect the financial position and results of operations of the enterprise which he has audited. It is most important not only that the CPA shall refuse consciously to subordinate his judgment to that of others, but that he avoid relationships which would be likely to warp his judgment even subconsciously in reporting whether or not the financial statements he has audited are in his opinion fairly presented. Independence in this sense means avoidance of situations which would tend to impair objectivity or create personal bias which would influence delicate judgments.

Sec. 15 — APPEARANCE AND REALITY

This special concept of the auditor's independence, though it underlies several provisions of the Institute's Code of Professional Ethics, is dealt with specifically only in Rule 1.01.*

Of crucial importance is the statement that independence is not susceptible of precise definition, but is an expression of the professional integrity of the individual. ("Integrity" here is used in the sense of uprightness of character, probity, honesty.) The reason that independence cannot be defined with precision is that it is primarily a condition of mind and character.

Generally, a reader of an opinion on financial statements may be expected to assume an independent state of mind on the part of the certified public accountant who signed it. But

*For complete text see page 183.

his confidence may be shaken if he learns that the auditor is involved in relationships which seem likely to impair objectivity. Thus it has been recognized that the appearance of lack of independence may be almost as damaging as the reality.

In the words of a former chairman of the Institute's committee on professional ethics:

> There are actually two kinds of independence which a CPA must have—independence *in fact* and independence *in appearance*. The former refers to a CPA's objectivity, to the quality of not being influenced by regard to personal advantage. The latter means his freedom from *potential* conflicts of interest which might tend to shake public confidence in his independence *in fact.**

Rule 1.01 recognizes this distinction in its insistence that the auditor *be* independent in fact. This is the reality. However, the rule goes on to say that the auditor must assess his relationships with his client to determine whether his opinion would be *considered* objective and unbiased by one who had knowledge of all the facts. In other words, he must not only *be* independent, but must not *appear* to be otherwise. The rule then states, but only as illustration, that a member of the Institute will be considered not independent if he expresses an opinion on the statements of an enterprise in which he has a financial interest or of which he is an officer, director or employee.

Even though a CPA knows that he *is* independent in a particular situation he is required to consider how he *seems* to others. He may not say with Hamlet, "Seems, madam! Nay, it is; I know not seems!"

However, no one can determine with certainty how a given

---

*Thomas G. Higgins, "Professional Ethics: A Time for Reappraisal," *The Journal of Accountancy*, March 1962, page 31.

situation might *seem* to any individual or group. Therefore, the rule of reason must prevail.

The committee on professional ethics has provided a rule of reason in an opinion which interprets Rule 1.01.* This opinion says in effect that the only relationships with a client which should lead to a member's being *considered* not independent are relationships which would suggest to a reasonable observer that a *conflict of interest* existed.

Even this criterion is quite general, but it is nevertheless helpful in dealing with specific cases, at least at the extremes of the spectrum.

For example, it seems safe to assume that if an auditor were a stockholder or director of a commercial corporation, reasonable observers would be likely to believe that a conflict of interest existed. They might ask how an auditor could be objective in expressing an opinion on results of operations if he were financially interested in those results, or if he had been part of the management whose decisions produced those results.

At the other extreme, the committee on professional ethics has said, for example, that normal professional or social relationships or the rendering of professional services other than the audit would not necessarily suggest a conflict of interest to a reasonable observer.

But in between the extremes there are some difficult questions.

Sec. 16 — MANAGEMENT SERVICES

For instance, a question has sometimes been raised as to whether the rendering of management services to a client is likely to impair a CPA's independence—in appearance or in reality—in expressing an opinion on the financial statements of

*Opinion No. 12, page 206.

the same client. The answer to this question has been that so long as the CPA confines his management services to advice, and does not participate in the final decision-making processes of the client, his independence need not be affected.

However, this position has been challenged.* The challengers contend that advising and decision-making cannot be separated and that the CPA who gives management advice cannot avoid participating in management decisions. It is said that management decisions are seldom made by one individual but are worked out by the company's staff and outside experts, including the CPA. Therefore, the CPA must sit in on the discussion that leads to the final decision to be sure that there have been no changes in circumstances which may affect the advice he gives. This situation, it is argued, results in such a mutuality of interest of the CPA and his client that the CPA ceases to be independent as auditor.

This argument should be tested against the basic assumptions regarding independence (1) in fact, and (2) in appearance.

It may be postulated that the CPA who renders management services will be no less independent *in fact* in his capacity as auditor than the CPA who does not. There is no basis for contending that his personal integrity will be affected.

The next question, then, is whether the performance of management services would seem to a reasonable observer to create a conflict of interest in relation to the audit function.

At this point it is necessary to determine what is meant by "management services." The term has not been authoritatively defined. It is conceivable that some unusual services to management might involve financial relationships or advice or decisions of a nature which could suggest a conflict of interest. But the ethical question must be considered in relation to the types of management services normally rendered by the largest

*See, for example, R. K. Mautz and Hussein A. Sharaf, *The Philosophy of Auditing*, American Accounting Association, University of Iowa, Iowa City, Iowa, 1961, Chapter 8.

numbers of CPAs—including, but not confined to, systems, cost analysis, budgeting, inventory control, and the like.

This problem is highlighted by a recent survey reported in the July 1965 issue of *The Accounting Review*.* Questionnaires were addressed to four carefully selected groups: (a) research and financial analysts of brokerage firms; (b) commercial loan and trust officers of banks; (c) investment officers of insurance companies; and (d) investment officers of domestic mutual funds.

The key question was, "Has the expansion of the CPA into the field of management consulting affected your confidence in his audit independence?"

In summary, some 43 per cent of the respondents did not believe that management consulting seriously endangers the CPA's independence; 33 per cent believed that it does; and 24 per cent were somewhat undecided.

But nowhere in the questionnaire or the article interpreting it is there a definition of the term "management consulting." This term may well evoke a reaction different from that evoked by "management services," which is commonly used by the profession itself. In any event, it cannot be assumed that all the respondents to the questionnaire were familiar with the specific services offered by CPA firms as aids to management. The respondents may have read into the question types of "consulting" which in fact are not commonly engaged in by CPAs.

It is difficult to believe that reasonable observers—stockholders, creditors or other users of financial statements, or the business public generally—would see any conflict of interest in the fact that the auditor, in addition to giving an opinion on the financial statements, also applied his technical knowledge and skill to the improvement of management's planning, control and decision-making processes.

---

*Arthur A. Schulte, Jr., "Compatibility of Management Consulting and Auditing," *The Accounting Review*, July 1965, p. 587.

As a matter of fact, advice and assistance in improving clients' accounting systems and internal controls have been normal functions of auditors from time immemorial—functions which have never raised any questions about independence.

Substantial benefits may result from combining the two functions. Knowledge of audit requirements can be useful in many types of management services, and the CPA must see to it that his recommendations meet the tests he would impose as auditor. Since management services are nonrecurring, the audit fees are likely to be more important to the accounting firm in the long run. A poor management services job may risk the loss of the audit, but this tends to improve the quality of the consulting rather than impair the independence of the auditor.*

As noted earlier in this chapter, it has been asserted that advising and decision-making are inseparable. To be sure, the line between the two may occasionally be difficult to draw. Nevertheless, it has been well established that the line does exist. The decision process has been broken down into the following steps:

1. Determining the nature of the decisions which could possibly be taken, i.e., delineating the possible acts.
2. Determining the set of events which could occur, and one of which must occur, which have an effect on the outcome of the operation.
3. Determining the expected profit or loss from each act-event combination.
4. Determining the probability of occurrence of each event.
5. Computing the expected value of each act and selecting the act with the highest expected value.

It has been contended, after analysis of a statistical decision model, that the CPA can freely participate in this process and

---

*Kenneth S. Axelson, "Are Consulting and Auditing Compatible?" *The Journal of Accountancy*, April 1963, pages 54-58.

still be considered independent, if he confines his advice to the first three steps shown above.* It is doubtful whether even the fourth step would suggest a conflict of interest to a reasonable observer.

On the negative side it has also been alleged that in rendering management services the CPA becomes, in effect, an employee of the client and therefore cannot also be independent as auditor. But it seems obvious that by giving advice and assistance to management the CPA, though he may perform the same function that an employee might perform, does not thereby become an employee.

> The distinguishing characteristic of an employee is not his function but his dependence on management. If he is fired, he is out of a job. The consultant, like the auditor, is not out of a job if he loses a client. He has other clients. This fact enables both consultant and auditor to be economically independent of the management they serve.
>
> Nor, by advising management, does the consultant become management. No matter how influential advice is, neither the offering of it nor the acceptance of it gives the adviser either the authority or responsibility of management.... **

As stated earlier, it is possible to conceive of circumstances in which the auditor who performs management services might not be considered independent. The ethics committee has said that management rarely surrenders its responsibility to make management decisions, but if the auditor makes such decisions his objectivity might be impaired.† The important point is that there is no basic incompatibility between the two functions. The auditor who also acts as consultant simply has one

---

*James Wesley Deskins, "Management Services and Management Decisions," *The Journal of Accountancy,* January 1965, pages 50-54.
**Axelson, *op. cit.,* page 56.
† Opinion No. 12, page 206.

more factor to assess in determining whether a reasonable observer would regard him as subject to a conflict of interest.

As in so many arguments, the absence of definition of terms causes semantic difficulties. "Management services" embraces a wide variety of activities, and the phrase means different things to different people. "Independence" is also susceptible to a variety of subjective interpretations.

It is clear that a measure of confusion has been engendered within the profession on this important matter. It has arisen partly because of a tendency to extend to the ultimate theoretical limits the concept that the auditor must not only *be* but also *seem* independent.

In their anxiety to demonstrate their capacity for self-discipline, and to maintain and increase public confidence, CPAs in recent years have become preoccupied with the question of appearances. In the effort to discourage relationships which might appear to a reasonable observer to create a conflict of interest the ethical restraints have been narrowed and tightened.

Up to now this has been all to the good. Certainly an auditor who was a stockholder or a director of a profit-making organization would appear to a reasonable observer to be subject to a conflict of interest. But concern with appearances should not confuse appearance with reality. Too much emphasis on relationships which might conceivably suggest a conflict of interest to the most suspicious observer may be a disservice both to the profession and the public.

The result might be to deprive clients of valuable creative contributions to improved management which their auditors, through their very familiarity with the clients' business acquired in the course of the audit, are in a better position than anyone else to make. To split the accounting profession into two segments—one a group of ivory-tower auditors who did nothing but attest to the fairness of financial statements, and the other a group of experts in management and tax problems—would not only reverse the natural trend of accounting practice which has evolved over a century of experience; it would also add substantially to the cost of providing business with all the professional accounting service it needs.

Criteria of independence should be tested against basic questions: (1) Will a specific relationship really tempt an auditor to subordinate his professional judgment, despite all the sanctions to the contrary? (2) Would it seem to reasonable observers to be likely to do so? (3) How would it affect the public interest? Who is likely to be hurt?

It will hardly be possible to develop detailed rules, applicable across the board in all conceivable combinations of circumstances, which would eliminate any possible question, however remote, as to an auditor's independence. Indeed, any such effort might create the impression that CPAs are so susceptible to temptation that their profession must not only protect the public against their weakness, but must protect them against themselves.

In the literal sense it is unrealistic to assume that anyone can attain absolute independence. No human being can free himself from all outside influences—from his environment, in effect. No one except a hermit can avoid the influences of his family, friends, what he reads and hears, and the attitudes and standards of his community.

To contend that a CPA acting as auditor should have no relations with his client except those involved in his work as auditor, for fear that the public might suspect a conflict of interest, would lead to an absurd situation. The auditor would be working in a vacuum. He would not have the benefit of intimate understanding of the organization or free and frank discussions with client personnel. He would lose touch with the real world. It might even be suggested that his fee should be paid by the government or some other outside agency, lest his independence be jeopardized by accepting compensation from the client!

The answer is to provide sanctions which will give the public maximum assurance that auditors will not subordinate their judgment or subject themselves to what reasonable observers would regard as conflicts of interest. This has been done. The Code of Ethics not only makes each CPA accountable for any relationship likely to suggest a conflict of interest, but also requires adherence to generally accepted auditing standards and generally accepted accounting principles, and full disclosure of material facts. Both the Institute and the Securities and Exchange Commission enforce these standards. The penalties for noncompliance are so severe that no CPA would be likely to expose himself to them knowingly.

Sec. 17 — TAX SERVICES

Is the auditor's independence impaired if he also renders tax services for his client? It is sometimes argued that the independent audit is a quasi-judicial function and that representation of a client before the Internal Revenue Service is an act of advocacy. How, it is asked, can the CPA be both judge and advocate?

The difficulty here is that the word "advocate" is an ambiguous term when used in connection with the practice of CPAs. It is generally assumed that a lawyer acting as advocate is a special pleader who is not necessarily bound to disclose facts which might be disadvantageous to his client. Advocacy, as it is commonly understood, assumes that each side puts forward its best arguments and leaves it to the other to probe for the weak spots. The judge and the jury are presumed to find the truth in the opposing arguments.

In this sense it does not seem appropriate to say that a CPA acts as an advocate in tax practice. He must, in the opinion of the ethics committee, "observe the same standards of truthfulness and integrity as he is required to observe in any other professional work. This does not mean, however, that

[he] may not resolve doubt in favor of his client as long as there is reasonable support for his position,"* The converse seems to be that without reasonable support he must disclose the position.

While the approach and duties of lawyers in most areas of practice are quite different from those of CPAs, whose position in expressing opinions on financial statements might roughly be described as "quasi-judicial" rather than that of an advocate, it seems significant that in tax practice the American Bar Association and the American Institute of Certified Public Accountants are not far apart in their view of the members' ethical responsibilities.

Opinion 314 of the ABA Committee on Professional Ethics, issued April 27, 1965, says in part:

> Similarly, a lawyer who is asked to advise his client in the course of the preparation of the client's tax returns may freely urge the statement of positions most favorable to the client just as long as there is reasonable basis for these positions. Thus where the lawyer believes there is a reasonable basis for a position that a particular transaction does not result in taxable income, or that certain expenditures are properly deductible as expenses, the lawyer has no duty to advise that riders be attached to the client's tax return explaining the circumstances surrounding the transaction or the expenditures.

The converse of this seems to be that if he does not believe there is a reasonable basis for the client's position, the lawyer should not support it unless the circumstances are disclosed. This parallels Opinion No. 13 of the Institute's ethics committee.

The ABA opinion goes on to say . . . "as an advocate before a service which itself represents the adversary point of view, where his client's case is fairly arguable, a lawyer is under no duty to disclose its weaknesses. . . ."

*Opinion No. 13, page 208.

The Internal Revenue Service might not concede that it represents an "adversary point of view." But in any event a CPA is likewise under no ethical disability in arguing for a position for which he has already determined there is reasonable support. Indeed, he does this before the SEC if items in financial statements on which he has expressed an opinion are challenged.

The ABA opinion also says:

> In all cases, with regard to both the preparation of returns and negotiating administrative settlements, the lawyer is under a duty not to mislead the Internal Revenue Service deliberately and affirmatively, either by misstatements or by silence or by permitting his client to mislead.

The AICPA opinion implicitly reaches the same conclusion in stating that a CPA must "observe the same standards of truthfulness and integrity as he is required to observe in any other professional work."

What this all seems to add up to is that *in fact* the CPA maintains his professional independence—in the sense of not subordinating his judgment—in his tax work as elsewhere. And his independence—in fact or appearance—in his role as auditor is not necessarily impaired by rendering tax service to the same client.

As in the case of management services, it is, of course, possible to conceive of situations in tax practice in which a CPA could be involved in relationships which to a reasonable observer would cast doubt on his independence as auditor. But there is no evidence that the customary, everyday tax services which most CPAs have been performing for nearly fifty years would raise such a question.

Each unusual case must be tested against the basic criteria already described in this paper, in the light of the circumstances peculiar to the given situation.

Sec. 18 — SEC RULE ON INDEPENDENCE

The Securities Act of 1933 and the Securities Exchange Act of 1934 require in most cases that financial statements included in registration statements filed under these acts be "certified . . . by an independent public or certified accountant."

The Securities and Exchange Commission, charged with the administration of these acts, established the meaning of "independent" as used in the statutes by the following rule:

(a) The Commission will not recognize any person as a certified public accountant who is not duly registered and in good standing as such under the laws of the place of his residence or principal office. The Commission will not recognize any person as a public accountant who is not in good standing and entitled to practice as such under the laws of the place of his residence or principal office.

(b) The Commission will not recognize any certified public accountant or public accountant as independent who is not in fact independent. For example, an accountant will be considered not independent with respect to any person or any of its parents or subsidiaries in whom he has, or had during the period of report, any direct financial interest or any material indirect financial interest; or with whom he is, or was during such period, connected as a promoter, underwriter, voting trustee, director, officer, or employee.

(c) In determining whether an accountant may in fact be not independent with respect to a particular person, the Commission will give appropriate consideration to all relevant circumstances, including evidence bearing on all relationships between the accountant and that person or any affiliate thereof, and will not confine itself to the relationships existing in connection with the filing of reports with the Commission.*

From this it appears that the Securities and Exchange Com-

*Rule 2-01, Regulation S-X.

mission and the organized profession are in substantial agreement as to the distinction between appearances and reality. In fact it was the SEC which first set up objective criteria by which a CPA could be considered to lack independence without the necessity of proving a "state of mind."

As a result of consideration of specific cases, the Commission has found many factual situations in which the certifying accountants could not be considered independent. These have been summarized in Accounting Series Releases No. 47 and 81. Other rulings dealing with independence have been issued subsequent to Release No. 81.

Representative examples of these situations may be summarized as follows:

1. An accountant took an option for shares of his client's common stock in settlement of his fee.
2. Using their own funds, the wives of partners in an accounting firm purchased stock in a client of the firm immediately prior to registration.
3. The accountant's wife owned stock in a proposed registrant.
4. A partner in an accounting firm acted as controller of the registrant.
5. The certifying accountant was the father of the secretary-treasurer of the registrant.
6. A certifying accountant organized a corporation which purchased property from the registrant, giving the registrant a purchase money mortgage.
7. The wife of an accountant had a 47½ per cent interest in one of the three principal underwriters of a proposed issue by the registrant.
8. A partner of an accounting firm acted as one of three executors of the will of a principal officer of a registrant and as one of three trustees of a trust established under the will. The principal asset of the trust was a substantial proportion of the voting stock of the registrant.

Previous rulings of the American Institute's committee on professional ethics suggest that the committee agrees that in all these situations the certifying accountants could not be considered independent.

While the SEC does not use the phrase "conflict of interest" in this context, it seems clear that the relationships in the preceding examples would suggest to a reasonable observer that conflicts of interest existed.

Sec. 19 — FINANCIAL INTEREST IN ENTERPRISE UNDER AUDIT

Rule 1.01 prevents an Institute member from having any financial interest in an enterprise which he audits. The pertinent part of the rule reads as follows:

> A member or associate will be considered not independent . . . with respect to any enterprise if he, or one of his partners . . . during the period of his professional engagement or at the time of expressing his opinion, had, or was committed to acquire, any direct financial interest or material indirect financial interest in the enterprise . . .

A certified public accountant may be *in fact* independent, even though he has a financial interest in an enterprise which he audits. However, he might not *appear* independent in the eyes of a reasonable observer in possession of the facts. Doesn't the size of the interest have any bearing on the question? Possibly. But because of the difficulty involved in determining materiality, it was decided to forbid a direct interest altogether.

One of the important purposes of the independent audit is to contribute to the maintenance of mutual confidence between corporate management on the one hand and investors and creditors on the other. This confidence might be impaired if it were known that the independent auditor had a financial interest in the enterprise, since the reported financial position and earnings on which he expressed a professional opinion might affect the value of his own interest, and he might therefore be exposed to influences on his professional judgment which could impair its objectivity.

Not only must the CPA performing or supervising the audit be independent, but so must all his partners. The responsibility of independence cannot be evaded by changing the partner in charge of the audit.

The phrase "during the period of his professional engagement" refers to the time that he is actually working on the audit. It does not include the period covered by the financial statements. This means that if a CPA had a financial interest in an enterprise during the audit period but disposed of it before undertaking the engagement, he would not necessarily be considered lacking in independence.*

It will be noted that the auditor will be considered lacking in independence if he has *any* direct financial interest or *material* indirect financial interest in his client.** This makes an important distinction between a "direct" financial interest and an "indirect" one. If a member owns stock in a company and later accepts an engagement to audit the company, he may not make his "direct" interest an "indirect" one simply by transferring ownership of the stock to his wife. In such circumstances he would still be considered to have the benefits of direct ownership and consequently be lacking in independence.

What then is meant by an indirect interest? The kind of situation the committee had in mind when it presented this rule for adoption was that of a partner of an accounting firm who owned shares in a mutual fund which in turn owned stock in a company audited by the accountant's firm. Under such circumstances the accounting firm would probably be

---

* It will be noted that this position differs from that taken by the Securities and Exchange Commission. See above, page 31.
**The Illinois Society of Certified Public Accountants forbids its members to have *any* financial interest in an audit client, direct or indirect.

considered independent, provided that the accountant's interest was not material either in relation to the mutual fund's holdings or to his own net worth.

Another type of situation the committee had in mind was a financial interest held by someone related to the accountant but not closely—not sharing the same household with him. Under such circumstances the accountant may be considered to have an indirect financial interest in the client, but if it is not material his independence as auditor need not be jeopardized.

Sec. 20 — AUDITOR AS OFFICER OR DIRECTOR

The portion of the rule pertinent to this section reads as follows:

> A member or associate will be considered not independent . . . with respect to any enterprise if he, or one of his partners . . . during the period of his professional engagement, at the time of expressing his opinion or during the period covered by the financial statements, was connected with the enterprise as a promoter, underwriter, voting trustee, director, officer or key employee.

There is an important difference between serving as a director of a client company and having a financial interest therein, insofar as the auditor's independence is concerned. If a member serves as director of an enterprise at any time during the period covered by the financial statements, he may not be considered independent as auditor simply because he resigns the directorship. If this were permitted, he would be reviewing the results of decisions in which he had a part. He would, in a sense, be auditing his own work. Consequently he would be considered to be lacking in independence.

Another part of the rule may be appropriately considered here. It reads as follows:

> The word "director" is not intended to apply to a connection in such a capacity with a charitable, religious, civic or other similar type of nonprofit organization when the duties performed in such a capacity are such as to make it clear that the member or associate can express an independent opinion on the financial statements.

The purpose of this exception is to enable a member to lend his name to a worthy cause, such as United Fund or Community Chest, but still retain the right to act as independent auditor of the organization when the duties performed as director are such that they do not affect the appearance of independence. This does not mean, of course, that the auditor of any nonprofit organization, such as a hospital or educational institution, may serve on the board of directors, if his duties are such as to suggest a conflict of interest to a reasonable observer.

This part of the rule has been subject to challenge. It has been said that the exception is not realistic because an auditor-director can be personally committed to the program of a charitable organization to such an extent that he will find it difficult to maintain an objective point of view.

It has been alleged further that there should not be one standard of independence for profit organizations and another for nonprofit organizations. Audited financial statements of hospitals and universities are used by banks and insurance companies as a basis for long-term financing just as those of profit-making companies are.

On the other hand, it can be contended that no reasonable observer would consider the auditor to be in a conflict-of-interest situation by serving as director of a nonprofit institution. The absence of the profit motive reduces the probability of client pressure. Assuming professional integrity what motivation would an auditor-director have to subordinate his professional judgment? The ethics committee presently has this matter under consideration.

Sec. 21 — RE-EXPRESSING OPINIONS

Rule 1.01 has the following to say about re-expressing opinions:

> In cases where a member or associate ceases to be the independent accountant for an enterprise and is subsequently called upon to re-express a previously expressed opinion on financial statements, the phrase "at the time of expressing his opinion" refers only to the time at which the member or associate first expressed his opinion on the financial statements in question.

The effect of this provision is that a member may become a stockholder or director of a corporation of which he was formerly the independent auditor and still be considered independent with respect to the prior periods. Subsequently, however, he would not be considered independent. In re-expressing an opinion the auditor would remain responsible for determining whether there had been subsequent events which substantially affected the statements on which his opinion was originally expressed.

The reason for this provision is clear enough, and it is consistent with SEC rulings covering similar circumstances.

Sec. 22 — AUDITOR AS BOOKKEEPER

In general, the SEC takes the position that the independence of a certifying accountant is impaired if he performs original work on the accounting records of a registrant. In such cases the Commission rules out not only work on the underlying records but also postings to the general ledger and the preparation of closing entries. Occasionally, however, the Commission has permitted independent accountants to assist in the maintenance of client records in such an emergency as the sudden resignation or death of key accounting personnel.

There is no question of the right of the SEC to take this position. The Commission has the responsibility of administering statutes designed to protect the interests of enterprises which are financed by the public distribution of securities. It is entitled to set up any reasonable safeguards which it believes would facilitate the achievement of this objective.

The Commission requires independent audits as a check on management's accounting—a second look. If the CPA, in writing up the books, makes the initial decisions as to classification and allocation of transactions, he is not likely to appraise these decisions critically when he audits the financial statements. The double check is likely to be lacking.

The Institute's committee on professional ethics has also considered the auditor-bookkeeper question in the light of Rule 1.01. The committee decided to endorse the following statement from the Institute publication "Special Reports—Application of Statement on Auditing Procedure No. 28":

> *Writing Up Records.* Small businesses often have inadequate records. The independent auditor may be required to write up the books or make numerous adjusting entries and prepare the financial statements. The independent auditor is not necessarily lacking in independence simply because he has performed these services. Although he often does make disclosure of work he has performed, disclosure of these services is not necessary if in the circumstances of a particular engagement the independent auditor considers himself to be, in fact, independent. If possible, the examination should be conducted by staff members who were not associated with the original accounting work.

It is to be noted that this does not say that if the auditor has done the write-ups, appearance of independence cannot be affected. It says only that if he has rendered these services he is not *necessarily* lacking in independence. In fact, the committee has held that an accounting firm could not be considered independent if a member of its staff was a client's resident auditor, authorized to sign checks, approve vouchers, recommend personnel changes, and perform other management functions.

In general, however, the Institute has taken the position that if a member merely writes up his client's accounting records, his independence as auditor of the same client need not be questioned. This position has been re-examined and upheld in the past. But many members still disagree with it and even now it is once again under scrutiny by the committee.

Sec. 23 — WHEN THE AUDITOR IS NOT CONSIDERED INDEPENDENT

Occasionally a CPA's client may not require audited statements accompanied by an opinion of an independent auditor. The CPA may be a director of, or have a financial interest in, the client company. In such circumstances the CPA may properly perform general accounting services for the company, and may even audit its records, even though he cannot be considered independent. However, since his name may be associated with the statements, he must be careful not to mislead the reader of his report as to his position.

In order to make the position clear, the committee on professional ethics has recommended that language like the following be used in this type of situation:

> Inasmuch as we have a direct financial interest in XYZ Company [or other reason] and therefore are not considered independent, our examination of the accompanying financial

statements was not conducted in accordance with generally accepted auditing standards. Accordingly, we are not in a position to and do not express an opinion on these financial statements.*

In the committee's view, this is *all* the disclaimer should say. The CPA should not describe the auditing procedures he has followed. Some have said that the language of this disclaimer is too restrictive. Surely the auditor, they say, should at least have the right to state what he has done and what he has not done, even though not considered independent. If the auditor is *in fact* independent, but holds a few shares in a closely held business in a local community, it has been argued that the restrictions of Opinion No. 15 are too rigid.

Since independence is not only an ethical standard, but along with competence and due care, is one of the general auditing standards as well, it is clear that a CPA cannot claim to have made an examination in accordance with such standards unless he can be considered independent.

The position taken by the committee on this point is strengthened by Statements on Auditing Procedure No. 33, which asserts (page 18) that the general standards are personal in nature and apply alike to the areas of field work and reporting.

Sec. 24 — CLIENT CONFLICTS OF INTEREST

The question occasionally arises whether the independence of a certified public accountant is impaired if he simultaneously renders professional services to two or more persons whose interests are, or may be, in conflict.

It is an accepted precept in the legal profession that a lawyer should not serve two clients whose interests conflict, and by analogy it is sometimes assumed that CPAs may not properly

---

*Opinion No. 15, page 209.

do so either. The soundness of the analogy, however, is questionable. Lawyers act as advocates, and a single lawyer could obviously not be the advocate for opposing views. But CPAs are in a sense communicators between conflicting interests—for example, between management and stockholders. That is why so much stress is laid on their independence. CPAs commonly serve without impropriety as independent auditors for two or more clients whose interests may be in conflict, such as competitors in the same industry.

However, there may be special circumstances in which the relationship should be disclosed to all concerned in order that there may be no misunderstanding.

In considering a related question the Council of the American Institute long ago held that an independent public accountant may properly undertake accounting or auditing engagements, on behalf of government agencies and others, involving the accounts of a regular client, provided his relationship to the various parties is fully disclosed.

Sec. 25 — OTHER RULES RELATING TO INDEPENDENCE

Rule 1.01 has been the only provision of the Code of Professional Ethics discussed in detail in this chapter. Other rules have a bearing on the independence of a certified public accountant: notably, Rule 1.04, dealing with contingent fees; Rule 2.02, pertaining to responsibility and disclosure in reports; Rule 2.03, dealing with opinions and disclaimers; Rule 3.04, pertaining to commissions, brokerage and fee-splitting; and Rule 4.04, dealing with occupations incompatible with public accounting. Since these rules involve other ethical questions, in addition to their relation to independence, they will be discussed separately in later chapters.

To sum up, independence has three meanings to the certified public accountant. First, in the sense of not being subordinate, it means honesty, integrity, objectivity and responsibility. Second, in the narrower sense in which it is used in connection with auditing and expression of opinions on financial statements, independence means avoidance of any relationship which would be likely, even subconsciously, to impair the CPA's objectivity as auditor. Third, it means avoidance of relationships which to a reasonable observer would suggest a conflict of interest.

In the language of Statements on Auditing Procedure No. 33:

> It is of utmost importance to the profession that the general public maintain confidence in the independence of independent auditors. Public confidence would be impaired by evidence that independence was actually lacking and it might also be impaired by the existence of circumstances which reasonable people might believe likely to influence independence. To *be* independent, the auditor must be intellectually honest; to be *recognized* as independent, he must be free from any obligation to, or interest in the client, its management or its owners.

Of all the utterances about the nature and significance of the concept of independence, none is more penetrating than the conclusion of an official statement of the Council of the American Institute, adopted in 1947. Its sentiments are as valid today as they were then:

> Rules of conduct can only deal with objective standards and cannot assure independence. Independence is an attitude of mind, much deeper than the surface display of visible standards. These standards may change or become more exacting but the quality itself remains unchanged. Independence, both historically and philosophically, is the foundation of the public accounting profession and upon its maintenance depends the profession's strength and its stature.

Chapter 4

THE PROFESSIONAL
ATTITUDE

P ROFESSIONAL men should not only be competent and independent; they should also place public service ahead of financial reward. Why should any group accept such an obligation? Because it is otherwise impossible to achieve recognition as a profession. Acceptance of this obligation is by definition the professional attitude.

Placing service ahead of reward does not imply an unrealistic lack of concern about making money. All professional men desire adequate incomes. But profit cannot be the dominant motive in a profession. If it were, by definition the vocation would be a business.

Without a professional attitude it is impossible for any vocational group, even when it possesses all the other attributes of a profession, to realize its maximum opportunities for service, and to attain the full satisfaction to be derived from public confidence and approval.

Sec. 26 — RECOGNITION AS A PROFESSION

When someone needs a type of service associated with the skills of a recognized profession, he turns to a member of that profession for help. A recognized profession tends to acquire an exclusive franchise in the field of work with which it is identified. In some fields, such as medicine and law, where the public health or welfare would be endangered if unqualified persons were permitted to practice, the profession's monopoly is granted by law and enforced by the courts. Other professional groups, including certified public accountants, acquire partial monopolies in some fields of work because the public interest would suffer if unqualified or undisciplined persons were permitted to do that kind of work.

In some states those who are licensed to practice public accounting are given the exclusive right to perform certain services. Unlicensed persons are prevented by law from assuming professional titles and from expressing opinions on financial statements. But even without benefit of legislation, the habits of the business and financial community have resulted in wide acceptance of the idea that certified public accountants should be engaged when professional opinions on financial statements are needed, or when other accounting service at a professional level is desired.

To the extent that a profession acquires either by law or by custom an exclusive privilege to do certain kinds of work, the members of that profession are freed from uninhibited competition. This permits concentration on improvement of the quality of service, encourages independence, and permits practice in an atmosphere of dignity and self-respect.

In our society, public respect is won most readily by those who do the most for others. Political and military leaders, great teachers and scientists, artists, outstanding industrial managers, labor leaders, professional men and other public servants are more honored than those who work only for their own enrichment.

Recognition as a member of a profession, then, satisfies two basic needs of man: It helps him make a living and it helps him win the respect of his fellows.

Certified public accountants have achieved wide recognition as a profession. However, their abilities and the importance of their work are still not fully understood. The day has not yet come when CPAs are universally recognized as a profession of the first rank, but the opportunities for the future are virtually unlimited.

Sec. 27 — THE ACCOUNTING PROFESSION AND
THE NEW SOCIETY

A new form of economy has arisen in this country. It might be called "supervised private enterprise." It attempts to combine the creative forces of competition in business with safeguards against exploitation of one group by another. Its objective is a higher standard of living for everyone. It requires ever-increasing productivity, which in turn calls for ever-increasing investments in labor-saving machinery. The system is made workable largely by imposing accountability on business management—accountability to stockholders, investors, creditors, government regulatory agencies, taxing authorities and others who have legitimate interests in the enterprise concerned.

Such a system creates many new opportunities for service by certified public accountants, who are recognized as experts in the measurement and communication of quantitative data, whose attestations add credibility to financial statements, and who are accepted as advisors to business management. Certified public accountants have so far only scratched the surface of their opportunities.

Sec. 28 — RULES ENCOURAGING THE PROFESSIONAL
ATTITUDE

Professional recognition comes from the public's reaction to
what members of the profession do—not to what they say
about themselves. To maintain and broaden public confidence
they must act like professional men—they must maintain a
professional attitude. They can never afford to take their
recognition for granted and become careless in their professional conduct.

In his book on the ethics of lawyers, Henry S. Drinker gives
the primary characteristics which distinguish the legal profession from business. Among them are the following:

1. A duty of public service, of which the emolument is a
by-product, and in which one may attain the highest eminence
without making much money. . . .

2. A relation to clients in the highest degree fiduciary.

3. A relation to colleagues . . . characterized by candor, fairness
and unwillingness to resort to current business methods of advertising, and encroachment on their practice, or dealing directly with their clients.*

These principles apply with equal appropriateness to certified public accountants. But generalizations are not enough.
The student and the young practitioner are entitled to guidance
on how to act in particular circumstances. One of the purposes
of the Code of Professional Ethics of the American Institute
of Certified Public Accountants is to provide such guidance.

No one suggests that a practitioner should pretend that the
making of a living is of no interest to him. He will not succeed
in creating the impression that he is primarily interested in

*Henry S. Drinker, *Legal Ethics,* Columbia University Press, New York, 1953,
page 5.

service unless it happens to be true. He should be clear in his own mind that he is interested first in doing a professional job and second in the compensation. He can do this without any disadvantage to himself, because experience shows that a professional man who concentrates on improving his capacity to serve need not be unduly concerned about earning money. The world will beat a path to his door.

One way of avoiding the impression that money-making is the primary interest is to avoid behavior commonly associated with commercial activities—for example, advertising, solicitation, and the giving and receiving of commissions.

The rules of conduct on these subjects are designed to encourage the professional attitude.

Compliance with them stamps the certified public accountant as a professional man.

Sec. 29 — ADVERTISING

The general prohibition against advertising is accepted today without much question. To be sure, there is nothing illegal or immoral about advertising as such, but it is almost universally regarded as unprofessional.

Younger accountants are sometimes tempted to advertise or solicit, and they may suspect that the rules are a result of a conspiracy among their older colleagues to protect themselves against new competition.

Actually the rule against advertising has many sound reasons to support it. In the first place, advertising would not benefit the young practitioner. If it were generally permitted, the larger, well-established firms could afford to advertise on a scale that would throw the young practitioner wholly in the shade. Secondly, advertising is commercial. Professional accounting service is not a tangible product to be sold like any commodity. Its value depends on the knowledge, skill and honesty of the CPA. Who would be impressed with a man's own statement that he is intelligent, skillful and honest? Lastly, advertising does not pay. The accountants in the early days who tried it agreed for the most part that it did not attract clients.

Rule 3.01 of the Institute's Code of Professional Ethics forbids advertising. It reads as follows:

> A member or associate shall not advertise his professional attainments or services.

> Publication in a newspaper, magazine or similar medium of an announcement or what is technically known as a card is prohibited.

> A listing in a directory is restricted to the name, title, address and telephone number of the person or firm, and it shall not appear in a box, or other form of display or in a type or style which differentiates it from other listings in the same directory. Listing of the same name in more than one place in a classified directory is prohibited.

Sec. 30 — CLASS OF SERVICE

Nothing is said in Rule 3.01 about the inclusion of descriptions on letterheads or elsewhere of classes of services rendered, such as audits, taxes, and systems. The committee on professional ethics, on the assumption that most people are aware of the usual services performed by CPAs, has interpreted Rule 3.01 to prohibit the association with a member's name of designations indicating special skills or the particular services he is prepared to render.* Previously the American Institute had agreed that a member should be prohibited from describing himself as a "tax consultant" or "tax expert" or from using any similar self-designation in the field of taxation.**

*Opinion No. 11, page 201.
**Opinion No. 5, page 193.

The result of these interpretations is that a member may not describe himself as a "tax expert," "management consultant," "bank auditor," etc., in directories, on his letterhead, business card, office premises, or anywhere else. Instead he may hold himself out simply as a "certified public accountant," a title which is thought to be sufficiently descriptive.

Even when the practice of a member is limited to specialized services, he may not indicate the nature of these services. In some cases members have formed partnerships with noncertified specialists in engineering, operations research, pension and profit-sharing plans, data processing, and other activities. Such partnerships, which would be precluded by law from using the CPA title, may not indicate the specialized services they are prepared to render.*

Sec. 31 — ANNOUNCEMENTS

The rule against advertising forbids only the publication of announcements or "cards" in newspapers or magazines. It does not prohibit the printing and mailing of such announcements to clients and friends. The committee on professional ethics has interpreted the rule to mean that "announcements of change of address or opening of a new office and of changes in partners and supervisory personnel may be mailed to clients and individuals with whom professional contacts are maintained, such as lawyers of clients, and bankers."**

Sec. 32 — DIRECTORY LISTINGS

Rule 3.01 is clear enough on the question of directory listings. Opinion No. 11 adds the information that if a classified direc-

*Opinion No. 17, page 211.
**Opinion No. 11, page 201.

tory has such headings as "Certified Public Accountants," or "Public Accountants," a member's name or that of his firm may appear under only one of these headings. The opinion says further that each partner's name, as well as the firm name, may be listed. For example, the firm name of Smith and Jones may appear under the heading "Accountants, Certified Public," and so may the individual names of John Smith and Robert Jones, despite the prohibition against listing the same name in more than one place. The reason for this latter restriction was primarily to prevent multiple listings frequently seen in classified directories under such headings as "Management Services," "Taxes," "Bookkeeping," and the like.

It is occasionally asked whether members may have listings in more than one directory. The ethics committee has ruled that listings are permitted only in the classified directories which cover the area in which a bona fide office is maintained. Because of the different standards of directory publishers throughout the country and because of geographical and other considerations, the committee has not attempted to say what an "area" includes but has left to the state CPA societies the task of defining the word.

Sec. 33 — "BOILER PLATE"

Some publishers print business newsletters, tax booklets and similar publications which might interest businessmen. These are offered for sale to CPAs, with imprint of the name and address of any CPA who may wish to send them to his clients.

In general, the Institute's committee on professional ethics does not wish to prevent members from sending any appropriate material to clients, but it does not approve the use of "canned" material when the appearance of the accountant's name on the publication might suggest that he prepared it.

The CPA need not have his name printed on material which he believes would be useful to his client. With better effect he might simply write a personal note to his client explaining why it is sent.*

Sec. 34 — DISTRIBUTION OF FIRM LITERATURE

Many CPA firms prepare and distribute, for the information of their clients and staff, publications bearing the firm's name, such as house organs, recruitment brochures, newsletters, and articles on tax, accounting, and business subjects. The ethics committee has no desire to curtail the production of such useful material, but it does insist that distribution be limited to those for whom the information was intended. If such publications fall into the hands of prospective clients, the firm which prepared them would be subject to criticism. The firm publishing the material is accountable for its distribution and even for its redistribution by others.**

Sec. 35 — INDIRECT ADVERTISING

The ethics committee has established the concept that a member may not do through others that which he is prohibited from doing directly. This principle applies with particular force to the restrictions on advertising and solicitation.†

Not only is a member prevented from causing others to carry out unethical activities on his behalf, but he also has a responsibility to see to it that they do not do anything that reflects discredit upon the accounting profession. It occasionally happens that a client in an excess of zeal will, in connec-

*Opinion No. 1, page 191.
**Opinion No. 9, page 197.
† Opinion No. 2, page 192.

tion with an advertising campaign, mention the name of his accountant and even extol his virtues. The member involved must put a stop to such advertising of his professional attainments and inform his client of the profession's rules.

However, it should be noted that if a CPA writes a book, his publishers may properly set forth the qualifications of the author. If the book deals with subjects on which Institute members are qualified to write, background information on the author, including his professional title and the name of his firm, may be mentioned by the publisher in advertising the work. However, the member himself is responsible for seeing to it that such promotional literature does not make statements that are not factual or in good taste.*

Sec. 36 — PRESS PUBLICITY

The rule against advertising is not intended to prevent public recognition of the personal achievements of a certified public accountant. Legitimate newspaper publicity about CPAs, including their firm names, is not advertising, but gratuitous recognition of something they have done which is of public interest. The Institute even encourages members to make statements on subjects which contribute to the public awareness of the profession.

Questions have arisen as to where the line should be drawn between legitimate publicity and unethical advertising. Articles have appeared in magazines and newspapers in which individual CPAs have been mentioned by name and their firms described in some detail. Such publicity may give such individuals or firms an advantage over other CPAs. Is it unethical for a CPA to cooperate with those who wish to give him this kind of publicity? Should he even permit it if he can prevent it?

*Opinion No. 4, page 193.

Institute members may certainly do things which attract favorable public attention; and there is little they can do to prevent the press and other media of communication from reporting their activities if they are of public interest. When a member learns that he is to be the subject of such news coverage, he should assist the author in assembling material so that the resultant articles are factually correct and directed to improving the image of the profession. However, in order to avoid advertising his own professional services or attainments, he should not give a writer or reporter information regarding the size of his firm, types of services which it renders, clients which it serves, location of offices, etc.

Despite the fact that the names of CPAs who may say and do things of public interest frequently appear in magazines and newspapers, it must be remembered that deliberately cultivated publicity with respect to professional attainments is taboo.*

Sec. 37 — SOLICITATION

Rule 3.02 of the Institute's Code of Professional Ethics reads as follows:

> A member or associate shall not endeavor, directly or indirectly, to obtain clients by solicitation.

If a professional man solicits an engagement, he places himself in a position psychologically inferior to that of the prospective client. In view of the CPA's responsibility to the public, as well as to his client, it is desirable that he and his client be on terms of equality. It is sometimes necessary for a CPA to tell his client what is good for him, as a physician

*Opinion No. 9, Sec. 4, page 199.

must tell his patient, whether he likes it or not. Occasionally, a certified public accountant finds it necessary to refuse to express an opinion on a statement in the form the client desires. It may be difficult for the CPA to preserve a position of independence if he has solicited the engagement in the first place.

There is no precise definition of solicitation. To write letters asking for work, openly or inferentially, or to ask for it orally, would certainly be solicitation. There is nothing improper, however, in a CPA's making himself known in his community by means of participation in civic or social affairs, by public speaking and by writing for various publications.

When overtures are made by a potential client, a certified public accountant is free to respond to them. The rule against solicitation does not prevent a CPA from discussing a possible engagement with anyone who broaches the subject, even though he is presently served by another public accountant. In fact, Rule 5.01 explicitly states that a member may furnish service to those who request it. When there is an incumbent accountant, however, it is considered good manners, and it is certainly good sense, for the CPA to defer acceptance of the engagement until the client has informed his present accountant of the decision to make a change. Then, with the client's knowledge, the CPA who is to succeed to the engagement will do well to speak to the predecessor frankly, informing him of the circumstances and leaving no lingering doubt as to who took the initiative in bringing about the change. This practice is no more than common courtesy. It is frequently followed and has engendered much goodwill among practitioners. It also may bring to light information which the CPA who is newly undertaking the engagement would be glad to learn.

The Institute's committee on professional ethics has, in the past, considered the desirability of adopting a rule that would require a member to notify the predecessor accountant that he has been asked to take over an engagement. This question will no doubt be the subject of further study in the future.

Sec. 38 — ENCROACHMENT

Related to the solicitation rule is Rule 5.01, which states in part that a member shall not encroach upon the practice of another public accountant. This rule will be discussed in detail in Chapter 9, but one important aspect of it may be considered here.

The fact that a CPA may not encroach upon the practice of another public accountant should not be interpreted to mean that a CPA may solicit an engagement when there is no incumbent accountant. The rule against solicitation applies with equal force whether or not the prospective client already has an accountant. Newly incorporated companies and others requiring the services of outside accountants for the first time are therefore not to be considered fair game for solicitation.

Sec. 39 — PERSONAL RELATIONS

Typically a CPA will form close personal friendships outside the profession. His relatives, neighbors and other intimates will be interested in his work and will ask him general questions about the services rendered by CPAs. Is the solicitation rule intended to prevent a member from responding to such questions? Certainly not. Nothing is more natural than for a man to talk at some length about what he does for a living. The solicitation rule was not intended to impede normal social intercourse. Needless to say, however, a CPA should not take the initiative in offering his professional services to social acquaintances.

Sec. 40 — HOW TO BUILD A PRACTICE

If a young practitioner, newly embarked upon a professional career, is not permitted to advertise his services or attainments or to solicit engagements, then how is he to obtain clients?

Actually, it is unwise to undertake public practice until one has a sufficient circle of friends and acquaintances in a community to justify the hope that announcements of the opening of an office will bring requests for professional assistance. After that, good work will lead to further requests. There is no advertisement like a satisfied client.

A newly established practitioner will often be recommended to others by his friends. Bankers, lawyers and other CPAs are in a position to do this. But a newcomer must be patient, and he must have enough capital to be able to wait for the first engagements. It takes time for a community to realize that a new CPA is in its midst.

Above all, the newly established practitioner should resist the temptation to throw himself in the way of clients of another firm of whose staff he was formerly a member. He met those clients as an employee of the other firm, and he will get off on the wrong foot if he seeks to lure them to his own office. If they approach him of their own volition, that is another matter.

Sec. 41 — COMMISSIONS, BROKERAGE AND FEE-SPLITTING

Rule 3.04 of the Institute's Code of Professional Ethics reads as follows:

> Commissions, brokerage, or other participation in the fees or profits of professional work shall not be allowed or paid directly or indirectly by a member or associate to any individual or firm not regularly engaged or employed in the practice of public accounting as a principal occupation.

> Commissions, brokerage, or other participation in the fees, charges or profits of work recommended or turned over to any individual or firm not regularly engaged or employed in the

practice of public accounting as a principal occupation, as incident to services for clients, shall not be accepted directly or indirectly by a member or associate.

The committee has held that this rule does not prevent a member from coordinating his work on a specific project for a single client with engineers, lawyers or members of other professions. In the event of such interprofessional cooperation, the member should ordinarily bill the client directly for his services.

The committee has also ruled that this provision of the Code was not intended to preclude payments to a retired partner of a public accounting firm or to the heirs or estate of a deceased partner.*

Nor does it at present prevent a practicing member from forming a partnership with a non-CPA. The committee has considered proposing a rule that would outlaw "mixed partnerships" but has not done so, though the matter is still on its agenda.

Maintenance of a professional attitude is one reason for the prohibition against giving or receiving commissions or brokerage, or splitting fees with nonpractitioners. Such practices are not reprehensible in others, but if a CPA engages in them, the public may suspect that he is more interested in making money than in giving service. This would weaken public confidence and the practitioner's prestige.

An equally important purpose of Rule 3.04, however, is to discourage conduct which might impair relations with clients. This aspect of the rule will be discussed in Chapter 8 (see page 137).

To sum up, the professional attitude demonstrates that the obligation to serve the public is accepted as a primary obligation, and that financial gain is relegated to second place. To

*Opinion No. 6, page 194.

gain public recognition as a profession it is necessary not only to accept that obligation, but to act in such a way that the public will believe it. This requires renunciation of many practices that are wholly acceptable in business, but which, if carried over into professional practice, would tend to make it indistinguishable from business, and would impair independence and the quality of professional service. The satisfactions and opportunities for service which come from recognition as a profession far outweigh any advantages which could be expected from abandonment of the professional attitude.

PART TWO

Auditing, Tax Practice, and Management Services

Chapter 5

OPINIONS ON
FINANCIAL STATEMENTS

SOME of the services which practicing certified public accountants offer in the fields of taxation and management aids may also be rendered by others. But only CPAs, and other public accountants when permitted by law, offer as a professional service to examine financial statements and express opinions for which they take professional responsibility as to the fairness of the presentation.

Sec. 42 — INDEPENDENT AUDITS

The demand for this professional service has resulted from the evolution of the free-enterprise economic system. Greater productivity and steadily improving technology have led to increasing demands for money to provide plants, machinery, working capital and the like, in amounts which could be obtained only by wide distribution of securities to the public, or by extension of credit on a scale far beyond the limits justified by personal acquaintance and personal responsibility.

The independent audit leads to the expression of a professional opinion as to whether financial information furnished to stockholders, prospective investors, bankers and other credit grantors, is fairly presented. Obviously the extent to which the opinion of a CPA on financial statements will add to their credibility in the eyes of investors or credit grantors will depend on their confidence in his independence of professional judgment, his technical competence and his assumption of an ethical responsibility to the public, as well as to his client.

Sec. 43 — COMPLIANCE WITH ACCOUNTING AND AUDITING STANDARDS

To strengthen public confidence, therefore, the Code of Professional Ethics of the American Institute of Certified Public Accountants includes many provisions which are designed to reinforce the auditor's independence. It also requires conformity with auditing standards, including the disclosure of all material facts.

Rule 2.02 helps to accomplish these purposes:

In expressing an opinion on representations in financial statements which he has examined, a member or associate may be held guilty of an act discreditable to the profession if:

(a) he fails to disclose a material fact known to him which is not disclosed in the financial statements but disclosure of which is necessary to make the financial statements not misleading; or

(b) he fails to report any material misstatement known to him to appear in the financial statement; or

(c) he is materially negligent in the conduct of his examination or in making his report thereon; or

(d) he fails to acquire sufficient information to warrant expression of an opinion, or his exceptions are sufficiently material to negative the expression of an opinion; or

(e) he fails to direct attention to any material departure from generally accepted accounting principles or to disclose any material omission of generally accepted auditing procedure applicable in the circumstances.

This one rule covers a lot of ground, but its effect is simply to require the independent auditor to do a workmanlike job, and to tell the truth, the whole truth, and nothing but the truth, without fear or favor.

Sec. 44 — GENERALLY ACCEPTED AUDITING STANDARDS

Rule 2.02 requires an auditor to disclose any material omission of "generally accepted auditing procedure." As a guide to the members in determining what auditing standards and procedures are generally accepted, the Institute's committee on auditing procedure has issued statements of auditing standards and a series of Statements on Auditing Procedure, which have now been consolidated into Statements on Auditing Procedure No. 33, "Auditing Standards and Procedures." Statements on Auditing Procedure No. 34 ("Long-Term Investments") was subsequently issued (September 1965).* The auditing committee recognizes that the authority of the statements rests on their general acceptability, but the burden of justifying departures from the committee's recommendations must be assumed by those who adopt other practices.

In some cases auditing standards and procedures have been formally adopted by the Council or membership of the Institute. The only auditing procedures presently having this status are those requiring observation of inventories and confirmation

* At this writing (October 1965) Statement 35 is about to be issued.

of receivables. However, the membership of the Institute has voted on and approved all ten of the "generally accepted auditing standards." These include three general standards (concerned with the personal qualifications of the auditor and the quality of his work), three standards of field work and four of reporting.*

> Auditing standards differ from auditing procedures in that "procedures" relate to acts to be performed, whereas "standards" deal with measures of the quality of the performance of those acts and the objectives to be attained by the use of the procedures undertaken. *Auditing standards* as thus distinct from *auditing procedures* concern themselves not only with the auditor's professional qualities but also with the judgment exercised by him in the performance of his examination and in his report.**

Sec. 45 — GENERALLY ACCEPTED ACCOUNTING PRINCIPLES

The Accounting Principles Board of the American Institute of Certified Public Accountants has been authorized by the Council to issue opinions on accounting principles on which financial statements are based. Since assuming the responsibilities of the former Institute committees on accounting procedure and on terminology in 1959, the Accounting Principles Board has issued six such opinions.

The committee on accounting procedure had issued 51 accounting research bulletins, of which eight dealt with terminology, and four additional terminology bulletins had been issued by the committee on terminology.† The Accounting Principles Board has authority to review and revise any of

---

*SAP 33, pages 15-16.
**Ibid., page 15.
†These are conveniently available in the 1961 Institute publication *Accounting Research and Terminology Bulletins* (Final Edition).

its own opinions and any of the bulletins of the predecessor committees. In 1965 the Board reviewed all existing accounting research bulletins issued by the former committee on accounting procedure and issued an Opinion amending some of these bulletins in some respects.* With these amendments, the older bulletins continue in effect with the same degree of authority as Board Opinions.

These opinions and bulletins are intended to provide objective standards to guide individual judgment and to minimize unnecessary variations in accounting principles which might result from purely subjective determinations.

The usual short form of an auditor's report embodies a clause that the financial statements have been prepared "in conformity with generally accepted principles." Rule 2.02(e) of the Code of Professional Ethics requires an auditor to direct attention to any material departure from "generally accepted accounting principles."

A special bulletin to members from the president of the American Institute of Certified Public Accountants** stated that the American Institute's Council in October 1964 adopted recommendations of a special committee that members should see to it that departures from opinions of the Accounting Principles Board (or accounting research bulletins) are disclosed, either in the footnotes to the financial statements or in the audit reports of members. This action applies to financial statements for fiscal periods beginning after December 31, 1965.

Council concluded that "generally accepted accounting principles" are those principles which have substantial authoritative support, that Opinions of the Accounting Principles Board constitute "substantial authoritative support," but that such

---

*Opinions of the Accounting Principles Board, No. 6, *Status of Accounting Research Bulletins,* October 1965.

**Thomas D. Flynn, "Disclosure of Departures from Opinions of Accounting Principles Board," October 1964.

support can also exist for accounting principles that differ from Opinions of the Accounting Principles Board.

If an accounting principle that differs materially in its effect from one accepted in an Opinion of the Accounting Principles Board is applied in financial statements, the reporting member must decide whether the principle has substantial authoritative support and is applicable in the circumstances. If he concludes that it does not, he would either qualify his opinion or give an adverse opinion as appropriate. If he concludes that it does have substantial authoritative support, he would give an unqualified opinion and disclose the fact of departure from the APB Opinion in a separate paragraph in his report or see that it is disclosed in a footnote to the financial statements, and, where practicable, its effects on the financial statements.

In concluding its recommendations Council pointed out that the committee on professional ethics and the Institute's legal counsel had advised that the present by-laws and Code of Professional Ethics would not cover an infraction of the Council disclosure recommendations. However, the special bulletin pointed out that Council's action had the force and effect of a standard of reporting practice, deviations from which should have the attention of the Institute's practice review committee.*

Sec. 46 — ANALYSIS OF RULE 2.02

The introductory clause of Rule 2.02 may require some comment. "Expressing an opinion" has replaced the older phrase "certifying financial statements," which CPAs have avoided

---

*In an information bulletin the practice review committee said that it was organized "to encourage compliance with generally accepted accounting principles and auditing standards and to eliminate, insofar as possible, substandard reporting practices through education and persuasion rather than by disciplinary action."

for many years because it implies precision inappropriate in areas of auditing and accounting where judgment is involved. The auditor does not "guarantee the accuracy" of financial statements as the word "certify" might imply. Using the information he obtains by an examination of reasonable scope, he expresses a professional opinion on the fairness of the representations made.

"Expressing an opinion on representations in financial statements" emphasizes that the statements and the items in them are representations of the client, not of the auditor. It is well established that balance sheets and statements of income and retained earnings are the client's own representation of financial position and the results of its operations. Financial statements agree with and are supported by books of account prepared by the client. The company must assume primary responsibility for the accounts and the statements. The auditor examines the statements by obtaining sufficient supporting evidential matter, through tests and other auditing procedures, the extent of which is partly determined by an evaluation of the existing system of internal control. The auditor expresses his independent opinion on the fair presentation of information shown in the statements.

Subsections (a) and (b) of Rule 2.02 are unmistakably clear. Deliberate omission or distortion of material information is inexcusable.

Subsection (c) says, in effect, not only that an auditor's failure to discover material omissions or misstatements will be ground for discipline if he was materially negligent in his audit, but that a materially negligent examination or report is in itself ground for discipline, even if the offender did not miss a material omission or misstatement. This is a warning that careless work will not be tolerated, regardless of whether or not it happens to have injurious consequences.

Subsection (d) is the result of instances which had come to notice in earlier years in which qualifications or exceptions in auditors' opinions related to so many, or such important, items in the financial statements or which involved such serious limitations as to scope of examination that the opinion on the fairness of the statements as a whole had little significance. Yet the mere appearance of a CPA's name in conjunction with even a qualified opinion might lend an unwarranted appearance of credibility to the statements.

Because of Subsection (e) an auditor may not plead that he has done his full duty by seeing to it that there was "full disclosure" of all material transactions in the financial statements, including footnotes thereto, regardless of whether the accounting was in accordance with generally accepted principles and whether the auditing included generally accepted procedures applicable in the circumstances.

For a more detailed discussion of these matters the reader should consult Statements on Auditing Procedure No. 33, "Auditing Standards and Procedures," published by the American Institute of Certified Public Accountants.

Nothing here written should be taken to mean that generally accepted accounting principles or auditing procedures have been fully codified, or that there is universal agreement on how they should be applied in all circumstances. There is still wide latitude for individual professional judgment, and the need for experienced judgment of this kind increases as business affairs become more complex. There is no manual in which the certified public accountant can find the answer to every question he encounters. What has happened is that broad limits have been placed on individual discretion. Certain basic concepts have received general acceptance, and these have become objective standards which curb the exercise of personal prejudice, whim or caprice, and penalize ignorance or incompetence.

The assumption of greater responsibility is the *quid pro quo* for wider recognition, public confidence, and increased opportunities for service. Essentially, Rule 2.02, by defining his responsibilities, fortifies the CPA's concern for his independence in auditing financial statements. It advertises his obligation not to yield to the influence of a client, to hide behind the authority of a regulatory body, or, within the framework of standards set by his own professional peers, to accept any other person's judgment as a substitute for his own.

Sec. 47 — ACCOUNTANT'S RESPONSIBILITY WHEN OPINION IS OMITTED

Sometimes CPAs perform accounting service for clients which does not lead to the expression of a professional opinion. The scope of the engagement may be limited by agreement with the client and, therefore, may not provide sufficient justification for an expression of opinion on the fairness of the financial statements as a whole. Again, even though his examination has been adequate, the certified public accountant may find his exceptions so material as to negative the expression of opinion and, therefore, under the terms of Rule 2.02(d), he may not express an opinion.

But if as a result of his examination he were to report to the client stating what he did and commenting on various items in the statements, without expressing any opinion on the financial statements as a whole, and without giving any explanation for the omission of an opinion, a reader of the "report" is likely to be left in doubt as to the extent of the responsibility which the CPA assumes.

Such a report might be submitted by the client to a banker or other credit grantor, or even to stockholders. The appearance of the CPA's name in conjunction with the financial statements might add to their credibility in the eyes of third parties to an extent unwarranted by the circumstances. However, the untrained reader might not be able to determine from his own analysis of the certified public accountant's report to what extent the CPA intended, or did not intend, to assume responsibility for the fairness of the financial statements as a whole.

Rule 2.03 was adopted to clear up this uncertainty. It reads as follows:

> A member or associate shall not permit his name to be associated with statements purporting to show financial position or results of operations in such a manner as to imply that he is acting as an independent public accountant unless he shall:
>
> (a) express an unqualified opinion; or
> (b) express a qualified opinion; or
> (c) express an adverse opinion; or
> (d) disclaim an opinion on the statements taken as a whole and indicate clearly his reasons therefor; or
> (e) when unaudited financial statements are presented on his stationery without his comments, disclose prominently on each page of the financial statements that they were not audited.

This rule states in effect that if a CPA is unable to express an opinion on financial statements, but his name is associated with the statements, he must say that he is unable to express an opinion and must explain why.

The "unqualified opinion," referred to in (a), may be expressed only when it results from an examination made in accordance with generally accepted auditing standards, and when the presentation conforms with generally accepted accounting principles applied on a basis consistent with the preceding period and includes all informative disclosures necessary to make the statements not misleading.

The "qualified opinion" mentioned in (b) should give a clear explanation of the reasons for the qualification. The accountant may refer in his report to a note to the financial statements that describes the basis for a qualification, but a qualification based upon the scope of the examination ordinarily should be covered in the auditor's report. In order that the qualification may be clear and forceful, use of the words "except" or "exception" is recommended, though when the outcome of a matter is uncertain, the phrase "subject to" may be appropriate.

The "adverse opinion" referred to in (c) is an opinion that the financial statements do *not* present fairly the financial position or results of operation in conformity with generally accepted accounting principles. "An adverse opinion is required in any report where the exceptions as to fairness of presentation are so material that in the independent auditor's judgment a qualified opinion is not justified. In such circumstances a disclaimer of opinion is *not* considered appropriate since the independent auditor has sufficient information to form an opinion that the financial statements are not fairly presented. Whenever the independent auditor issues an adverse opinion, he should disclose *all* the substantive reasons therefor . . ."*

As for (d), when the auditor has not obtained sufficient information to form an opinion on the fairness of presentation of the financial statements, he should state in his report that he is unable to express an opinion on the statements and give all substantive reasons for his disclaimer. When he believes that the financial statements are false or misleading, he should, in the opinion of the ethics committee, require adjustment of the accounts or disclosure of the facts, and failing this he should refuse to permit his name to be associated with the statements in any way.**

The unaudited statements, referred to in (e), should be clearly and conspicuously marked on each page as unaudited. It is preferable that a disclaimer accompany all such statements; when they are accompanied by comments the auditor *must* issue a disclaimer of opinion.†

SAP 33, page 59.
**See Opinion No. 8, page 197.
† The foregoing paragraphs constitute a summary of *SAP 33*, pages 58-60.

Sec. 48 — RESPONSIBILITY FOR COMPLIANCE WITH
REQUIREMENTS OF GOVERNMENT BODIES

Government agencies which require audits of financial statements of enterprises subject to their jurisdiction often promulgate rules or regulations containing special requirements related to auditing, presentation of financial data, or reporting.

The Institute's Council has held that a member undertaking an examination is charged with the responsibility of familiarizing himself with accounting or auditing requirements of government agencies empowered to prescribe rules to which the client is subject.

If a certified public accountant finds that these requirements have not been fairly met in the financial statements and issues a report to be submitted to the government body, he must state the facts and take a clear exception as to conformance with the regulations. However, he may not accept government requirements as a substitute for generally accepted accounting principles. In general, such principles apply to enterprises whose accounting practices are prescribed by government regulatory authorities or commissions. Accordingly, material variances from generally accepted accounting principles should be dealt with in the CPA's report in the same manner followed for companies which are not regulated.*

Sec. 49 — FORECASTS

Certified public accountants are often asked to assist in the preparation of estimates of earnings contingent upon future transactions, of the type issued in prospectuses for new issues of securities, giving effect to the expected result of the new financing. Sometimes CPAs are asked to permit their names to be used in conjunction with such estimates or forecasts

*SAP 33, pages 70-71.

A CPA should not permit his name to be associated with any forecast of the results of future transactions unless he makes proper explanation.

Rule 2.04 of the Code of Professional Ethics says:

> A member or associate shall not permit his name to be used in conjunction with any forecast of the results of future transactions in a manner which may lead to the belief that the member or associate vouches for the accuracy of the forecast.

The reasons for this rule are evident. Opinions of CPAs on financial statements showing current financial position and the results of past operations, based on adequate examination, are relied upon to an extent which indicates a high degree of public confidence.

The CPA certificate has acquired such prestige that the appearance of the name of a certified public accountant in conjunction with financial data inevitably adds credibility.

Public confidence would be impaired if certified public accountants commonly permitted their names to be used in conjunction with forecasts of the results of future transactions, or other data not susceptible of adequate substantiation.

Budgets, cost analyses, and other financial data prepared primarily for the use of business management might be submitted to banks or other credit grantors as evidence of financial responsibility. The ethics committee has held that it is entirely proper for members to assist clients in the preparation of pro forma statements of financial position and results of operation, cost analyses, budgets and other similar special purpose financial data, which set forth anticipated results of future operations. However, when a member's name is associated with such material he must disclose the source of the information used and the major assumptions made, and he must indicate that he does not vouch for the accuracy of the forecast.*

*See Opinion No. 10, page 200.

There is a certain ambiguity in the phrase "vouch for the accuracy of the forecast." This does not, of course, refer to the accuracy of the mathematical computations but rather to whether or not the prediction itself will come true.

Sec. 50 — use of cpa's name by another

Two provisions of the Code of Professional Ethics are intended to prevent a member from serving as a "front" for another accountant over whose work the member does not exercise adequate supervision and control. The first of these is Rule 2.01:

> A member or associate shall not express his opinion on financial statements unless they have been examined by him, or by a member or employee of his firm, on a basis consistent with the requirements of Rule 2.02.
>
> In obtaining sufficient information to warrant expression of an opinion he may utilize, in part, to the extent appropriate in the circumstances, the reports or other evidence of auditing work performed by another certified public accountant, or firm of public accountants, at least one of whom is a certified public accountant, who is authorized to practice in a state or territory of the United States or the District of Columbia, and whose independence and professional reputation he has ascertained to his satisfaction.
>
> A member or associate may also utilize, in part, to the extent appropriate in the circumstances, the work of public accountants in other countries, but the member or associate so doing must satisfy himself that the person or firm is qualified and independent, that such work is performed in accordance with generally accepted auditing standards, as prevailing in the United States, and that financial statements are prepared in accordance with generally accepted accounting principles, as prevailing in the United States, or are accompanied by the in-

formation necessary to bring the statements into accord with such principles.

In earlier days cases were reported in which noncertified accountants had obtained engagements in which it was necessary that opinions expressed on financial statements be signed by a CPA. In such a situation, the noncertified accountant might approach a CPA friend and offer him a portion of the fee for signing the report. Clearly it would not only be unethical for the CPA to do so, but he might expose himself to severe legal liabilities.

No certified public accountant would wish to put himself in such an equivocal position and the instances have undoubtedly been rare in which such offers have been accepted. However, Rule 2.01 serves to put the public on notice that when the name of a member of the Institute appears, it may be assumed that he has either supervised the work or satisfied himself that it was competently performed by another qualified accountant, and that the member assumes responsibility for it.

Quite properly, the rule permits collaboration among qualified and accredited professional accountants or accounting firms in conducting parts of an engagement or related engagements. For example, firm X, composed of CPAs examining the accounts of Blank corporation, whose main offices are in New York, may request firm Y, also composed of CPAs, to observe the taking of the physical inventory of the corporation's California branch. Firm Y submits its report of the inventory, for which it assumes professional responsibility, to firm X, and the latter is entitled to utilize it, to incorporate the Y report in its working papers, and to express an opinion on the financial statements of the corporation as a whole, in which the California branch inventory is incorporated. This type of collaboration is quite common. It saves time and travelling expenses. It is wholly proper and desirable.

To all intents and purposes, firm Y in this situation serves as an agent of firm X. The instructions as to how the examination of the branch office inventory is to be conducted are provided by X. Y's report is submitted to X, not to the client. Y is compensated for its work by X, not by the client. Y's name does not appear in the report. X assumes control of, and responsibility for, the entire engagement, but for the time being utilizes the work of firm Y as though it were a branch office of firm X. This is permitted, it will be noted, only if firm Y is composed of CPAs (in part at least) or qualified foreign accountants whose independence and professional reputation have been ascertained.

An extension of the same procedure commonly occurs in the examination of large corporations with numerous subsidiary companies, which publish consolidated financial statements. In such a case the accounting firm responsible for the entire engagement generally examines the accounts of the parent corporation, and ordinarily those of the subsidiaries which are geographically accessible. However, it sometimes happens that a recently acquired subsidiary prefers to have its work done by auditors whom it had retained when it was independent of the present parent. If these auditors are certified public accountants, Rule 2.01 permits the firm expressing an opinion on the consolidated statements to utilize the work of its colleagues with respect to the subsidiary, and incorporate its accounts in the consolidation—always provided that the firm satisfies itself that the work has been performed in accordance with accepted standards.

Again, when American corporations have subsidiaries or branches abroad, the auditors expressing an opinion on the consolidated statements may utilize statements attested to by qualified and independent foreign public accountants, provided their work is performed in accordance with the generally accepted auditing standards and the statements are prepared in conformity with the generally accepted accounting principles as prevailing in the United States; and may incorporate the foreign accounts in the consolidation — again provided that the auditors have satisfied themselves as to the standards under which such work was performed.

The other rule regarding the use of a certified public accountant's name by another is Rule 4.02. It reads as follows:

> A member or associate shall not practice in the name of another unless he is in partnership with him or in his employ, nor shall he allow any person to practice in his name who is not in partnership with him or in his employ.
>
> This rule shall not prevent a partnership or its successors from continuing to practice under a firm name which consists of or includes the name or names of one or more former partners, nor shall it prevent the continuation of a partnership name for a reasonable period of time by the remaining partner practicing as a sole proprietor after the withdrawal or death of one or more partners.

This rule is intended to prevent arrangements which in the earlier days of the accounting profession were not uncommon. A CPA might enter into an agreement with an accountant who was not certified and share the expenses of maintaining a joint office, without sharing in professional fees, or without a partnership agreement. The two names might appear on the office door. The noncertified accountant might represent that he was associated with the CPA.

A client or prospective client could be misled by the appearances to believe that the two accountants were partners. Credit grantors and others might assume that the certified public accountant accepted responsibility for, or exercised some supervision over, the work of the other accountant.

The rule makes it clear that not only is a member prohibited from hiding behind the name of another, but that such member shall not allow anyone who is not his partner or his employee to hide behind *his* name.

The portion of the rule pertaining to partnership names is discussed in Chapter 10, "Forms of Organization and Description," page 165.

Sec. 51 — SEC RULES AND OPINIONS ON FINANCIAL STATEMENTS

In addition to the rules of the Institute, state CPA societies, and state accountancy boards, the Securities and Exchange Commission has issued regulations relating to the professional responsibility of auditors expressing opinions on financial statements of enterprises subject to the jurisdiction of the Commission.

Rule 2-01 of Regulation S-X has already been quoted (see above, page 31). The remaining pertinent regulations are as follows:

Rule 2-02. Accountants' Certificates.

(a) Technical requirements. The accountant's certificate shall be dated, shall be signed manually, and shall identify without detailed enumeration the financial statements covered by the certificate.

(b) Representations as to the audit. The accountant's certificate (i) shall state whether the audit was made in accordance with generally accepted auditing standards; and (ii) shall designate any auditing procedures generally recognized as normal, or deemed necessary by the accountant under the circumstances of the particular case, which have been omitted, and the reasons for their omission.

Nothing in this rule shall be construed to imply authority for the omission of any procedure which independent accountants would ordinarily employ in the course of an audit made for the purpose of expressing the opinions required by paragraph (c) of this rule.

(c) Opinions to be expressed. The accountant's certificate shall state clearly: (i) the opinion of the accountant in respect of the financial statements covered by the certificate and the accounting principles and practices reflected therein; (ii) the opinion of the accountant as to any material changes in accounting principles or practices or method of applying the accounting principles or practices, or adjustments of the accounts, required to be set forth by rule 3-07; and (iii) the nature of, and the opinion of the accountant as to, any material differences between the accounting principles and practices reflected in the financial statements and those reflected in the accounts after the entry of adjustments for the period under review.

(d) Exceptions. Any matters to which the accountant takes exception shall be clearly identified, the exception thereto specifically and clearly stated, and, to the extent practicable, the effect of each such exception on the related financial statements given.

Rule 2-03. Certification by Foreign Government Auditors.

Notwithstanding any requirements as to certification by independent accountants, the financial statements of any foreign governmental agency may be certified by the regular and customary auditing staff of the respective government, if public financial statements of such governmental agency are customarily certified by such auditing staff.

Rule 2-04. Certification of Financial Statements of Persons Other Than the Registrant.

If a registrant is required to file financial statements of any other person, such statements need not be certified if certification of such statements would not be required if such person were itself a registrant.

Rule 2-05. Certification of Financial Statements by More Than One Accountant.

If, with respect to the certification of the financial statements of any person, the principal accountant relies on an examination made by another independent public accountant of certain of the accounts of such person or its subsidiaries, the certificate of such other accountant shall be filed (and the provisions of rules 2-01 and 2-02 shall be applicable thereto); however, the certificate of such other accountant need not be filed (a) if no reference is made directly or indirectly to such other accountant's examination in the principal accountant's certificate, or (b) if, having referred to such other accountant's examination, the principal accountant states in his certificate that he assumes responsibility for such other accountant's examination in the same manner as if it had been made by him.

In 1917 the American Institute prepared a "memorandum on balance-sheet audits," which was later published under the title, "Uniform Accounting: A Tentative Proposal Submitted by the Federal Reserve Board." This was the first of a long series of documents inspired by the organized profession and devoted to the improvement of auditing and reporting standards. These publications include, among others, statements on auditing procedures and standards, booklets on specific areas of auditing prepared by Institute committees, and case studies on auditing problems published by the Institute's staff. All of these give a clear indication of the extent to which CPAs are willing to discipline themselves in the interests of the financial community and of the public. The profession has every right to be proud of its record in this vital area of practice.

Chapter 6

TAX PRACTICE

A REAS of tax practice in which most CPAs most frequently engage include assistance to taxpayers in determination of tax liabilities and in planning business transactions with a view to tax effects; preparation of tax returns and claims for refund; processing requests for rulings and applications for exemption; representation of taxpayers in discussion of returns with examining agents and in settlement of proposed additional assessments or claims for refund with the Internal Revenue Service.

It has been estimated that tax practice produces as much as one quarter of the fees of the accounting profession. The CPA's work in taxes has been one of the reasons for the rapid growth of the profession. Individuals and businessmen must keep careful accounts in order to comply with income tax requirements. This has stimulated the demand for accounting services, particularly the installation of systems which yield the information necessary to prepare and support tax returns.

In auditing and management services the CPA's clients are usually business enterprises or institutions. But in tax work CPAs also serve large numbers of individuals. This wide acceptance of the CPA as a tax advisor has contributed substantially to the successful administration of the income tax laws— often described as a voluntary self-assessing tax system.

Thus in tax practice the CPA again finds himself in a position of multiple responsibilities. He obviously has a primary duty to his client. But he must also recognize an obligation to the government and to the public which it represents.

CPAs assist hundreds of thousands of taxpayers in the preparation of returns. Most businesses, as well as many individuals, need such help. However, the Treasury Department places no limitation on who may prepare tax returns for another. Many lawyers, noncertified accountants and others also engage in this work. Anyone giving a taxpayer such assistance must sign a preparer's declaration incorporated in the return, if a fee was charged.

Lawyers and certified public accountants, by virtue of their professional status alone, are admitted to practice before the Treasury Department — i.e., to represent taxpayers in dealings with the Internal Revenue Service. Others may be enrolled as "agents" to practice before the department by passing an examination for the purpose, or by virtue of being former IRS employees.

In August 1965 there were approximately 89,000 persons enrolled to practice before the Treasury Department. Of these, about 44,000 were attorneys, 39,000 were CPAs, and 6,000 were qualified by virtue of former employment with the Internal Revenue Service or by means of the special enrollment examination.

Important ethical considerations arise continually in tax practice. Yet, the Institute's Code of Professional Ethics, which deals so thoroughly with the ethical responsibilities of the CPA as independent auditor, and in this area is backed up by a substantial literature, is virtually silent with respect to his ethical responsibilities in tax practice.

However, members of the American Institute of Certified Public Accountants have been disciplined by the Institute's Trial Board for improper conduct in tax practice under the general provision of the by-laws providing for suspension or expulsion for "conduct discreditable to the profession."

Even though tax practice is not identified prominently in the Code,* there can be no question that the Code does apply to tax practice. The ethics committee has made this explicit in Opinion No. 13, which reads as follows:

> It is the opinion of the committee that the Code of Professional Ethics applies to the tax practice of members and associates except for Article 2, relating to technical standards, and any other sections of the Code which relate only to examinations of financial statements requiring opinions or disclaimers.

> The committee is of the opinion that the statement, affidavit or signature of preparers required on tax returns neither constitutes an opinion on financial statements nor requires a disclaimer within the meaning of Article 2 of the Code.

> In tax practice, a member or associate must observe the same standards of truthfulness and integrity as he is required to observe in any other professional work. This does not mean, however, that a member or associate may not resolve doubt in favor of his client as long as there is reasonable support for his position.

In addition, Section 10.21(a) of Treasury Department Circular No. 230 provides in part that enrolled agents who are

---

*It is referred to only in Rule 1.04, which forbids fees contingent upon the findings or results of professional service but makes an exception in the case of Federal, state, or other taxes, in which the findings are those of the tax authorities, not of the accountant. (See Chapter 8, pages 138-143.)

CPAs shall conduct themselves and their practice before the IRS in accordance with recognized ethical standards applicable to CPAs generally.

Since the preparation of a tax return involves the measurement and communication of financial data—the determination of income under special rules—it is clearly a part of the accounting function. But a tax return is not a financial statement in the sense contemplated by Rules 2.02 and 2.03 of the Institute's Code. Nor is the signing of the preparer's declaration an expression of opinion in the sense contemplated by the profession's reporting standards. In signing a tax return as preparer the CPA says that to the best of his knowledge and belief it is true, correct, and complete, but this does not necessarily imply that he has made an examination of the underlying data.

However, the return preparer may not use lack of knowledge as a means of evading responsibility when he suspects that information submitted by the client is misleading, incorrect or incomplete. If upon questioning the client he learns that the information is faulty, he should not sign the return.

Some practitioners have attached disclaimers to the standard form of affidavit, pointing out that they have not examined the underlying data and accept no responsibility for the accuracy thereof. Opinions differ as to the effectiveness and desirability of such disclaimers. Internal Revenue Service personnel probably do not attach any significance to such disclaimers because they do not assume in any case that the practitioner has a responsibility to examine underlying data. Obviously nonaccountant preparers are not equipped to do so.

Yet, even sophisticated observers are sometimes surprised to learn that a CPA may prepare a return in sole reliance upon data submitted by the taxpayer. This is doubtless because the signature of a CPA has become so widely accepted as adding credibility to financial data. But it is only reasonable for the government to permit tax practitioners to rely, in good faith, upon information furnished by their clients, as long as there is no reason to suspect its validity. To require every return to be audited before the required declaration could be signed would impose a heavy burden on taxpayers. Yet the CPA, because of his professional identification as an auditor, is in a peculiar position: While he is not obliged to check all the information furnished to him, he may be criticized for failure to make reasonable inquiries if he had any reason to believe that the available information was not "true, correct and complete." Absence of direct knowledge does not justify ignoring indirect indications that information presented by a taxpayer may be false or misleading. In fact, many practitioners subscribe to the following view, expressed by a former chairman of the Institute's committee on professional ethics:

> It seems to me that any CPA who values his reputation for reliability and integrity should perform at least some minimum procedures of review and investigation before he is willing to sign as the preparer of the return.*

Against this general background of tax practice it is convenient to consider the CPA's ethical responsibility (1) to his client, (2) to the government, and (3) to the general public.

Sec. 52 — ETHICAL RESPONSIBILITY TO CLIENT
IN TAX PRACTICE

Determination of Tax and Preparation of Returns. In tax practice, as in other fields of practice, the CPA has a primary responsibility to his client. One duty to the client is to help

---

*Thomas G. Higgins, "Professional Ethics: A Time for Reappraisal," *The Journal of Accountancy*, March 1962, page 34.

him keep his tax to the minimum legally due—that is, to avoid unnecessary overpayment. The certified public accountant is not an agent of the government. The CPA, writes a former chairman of the Institute's committee on Federal taxation, ". . . is not expected to approach uncertain tax questions with the same lack of bias that he must apply in expressing an opinion on the fairness of presentation of a financial statement."[*]

The CPA also owes the client a duty to keep him out of trouble—to advise him to avoid underpayments of tax that may lead to interest or penalties, and particularly to dissuade him from concealments which might result in charges of fraud.

Unscrupulous tax practitioners, it has been said, have prepared returns deliberately which have resulted in overpayment of tax without the client's knowledge, in order that the practitioner might later get the credit, and perhaps an additional fee, for obtaining a refund. Unscrupulous practitioners have also encouraged clients to make questionable deductions which resulted in immediate tax "savings," for which the client was glad to pay the practitioner's fee, but which were offset later by additional assessments plus interest and penalties. These are clearly unethical practices for which an Institute member would be liable to discipline under the provisions of the by-laws relating to "conduct discreditable to the profession."

Discovery of Understatement in Prior Years. CPAs occasionally discover that a client, whether intentionally or not, has substantially understated income in prior years. On this point Treasury Department Circular No. 230, Section 10.23, has the following to say:

> Each enrolled attorney or agent who knows that a client has not complied with the law, or has made an error in or omission from any return, document, affidavit, or other paper which

---

[*]Thomas J. Graves, "Responsibility of the Tax Advisor," *The Journal of Accountancy,* December 1962, page 35.

the client is required by law to execute, in connection with any matter administered by the Internal Revenue Service, shall advise the client promptly of the fact of such noncompliance, error, or omission.

If the CPA believes that the client's error was intentional, he should remind the client that his civil rights may be involved. He should point out that as a CPA he does not have the legal right of "privileged communication," and consequently might be required to testify on statements made to him by the client, and to make available working papers, correspondence and other documents relating to the tax returns under consideration. He should therefore suggest that the client obtain legal counsel.

Neither the profession's rules nor the income tax laws or regulations require a return preparer to notify the Treasury Department of an error discovered in the return of a prior year. In fact, Institute members are expressly precluded from such action by Rule 1.03, which provides that a member shall not violate the confidential relationship between himself and his client.*

If a client refuses to take steps to correct an error in the return of a prior year, the CPA should consider withdrawing from the engagement, thus dissociating himself from participation in what may be a criminal act.

According to Section 10.24 of Treasury Department Circular No. 230, enrolled attorneys and agents are required to exercise "due diligence" in preparing and filing returns. The "diligence" is to be exercised in the *preparation* of the return, not in *investigating* the information submitted by the taxpayer.**
The Treasury Department does not consider that this "due diligence" requirement applies to CPAs in any special sense. In

---

*This rule is discussed in Chapter 8, pages 131-132.
**Graves, *op. cit.*, page 37.

other words, it applies across the board, to all tax practitioners, accountants and nonaccountants alike. Thus it could not reasonably be interpreted to require CPAs to make more extensive examinations of underlying data than other return-preparers.

Alternative Methods. Another recurring problem in the preparation of returns is how to present an unusual item of income or expense when alternative methods appear to be permissible under the Internal Revenue Code or related regulations, decisions, and rulings—and one method is better for the taxpayer than another.

First, it should be clear that there is nothing reprehensible in a CPA's assisting his client to minimize taxes by every legal means. In the words of Judge Learned Hand, "Over and over again courts have said that there is nothing sinister in so arranging one's affairs as to keep taxes as low as possible. Everybody does so, rich and poor; and all do right, for nobody owes any public duty to pay more than the law demands; taxes are enforced exactions, not voluntary contributions. To demand more in the name of morals is mere cant."

Where there is reasonable support for a position that will result in a lower tax for his client, the tax practitioner may not only advance the solution which is most favorable to his client, but it is his duty to do so. At the same time, he should make clear to the client the possibility that the most favorable method might later lead to a deficiency assessment and ultimately to litigation. The decision should be up to the client, not to the tax advisor, in view of the possibility of interest charges and penalties and the cost of possible controversy and litigation.

Sec. 53 — RESPONSIBILITY TO THE GOVERNMENT

A certified public accountant enrolled to practice before the Treasury Department may represent his client in negotiations with the Internal Revenue Service for the purpose of settling additional assessments or claims for refund. How much information should the CPA voluntarily reveal to the government agent? How much and what kind of information is he entitled to be silent about in the interest of reaching the best settlement which the CPA honestly believes the law allows? If the taxpayer has decided to report the transaction in a manner most favorable to him, and the CPA representing him believes it to be justifiable, is he under any obligation to bring to the attention of the Revenue Agent the possible alternative interpretations, or may he assume that the agent sustains the full burden of disproving the taxpayer's contention?

These are difficult and important questions, the answers to which may not yet be final. However, current thinking seems to be going along the following lines.

The IRS examining agent has every opportunity to inquire into the facts for himself and to request the information he desires. The practitioner is required to produce the documents and records called for, unless he has good reason for believing that the request is without foundation. In honoring direct requests of the examining agent, however, the practitioner has no obligation to volunteer information on matters which might reasonably be dealt with in alternate ways.

This approach has important implications for tax planning. In recommending to his client a course of action intended to secure certain tax benefits, the practitioner should try to foresee whether he will be able to answer frankly the questions of an IRS agent without threatening the proposed benefits. If he cannot, then he should probably not proceed with the plan.

Sec. 54 — RESPONSIBILITY TO THE PUBLIC

It must be recognized that the general public as well as the government is affected by the administration of the tax laws. If one citizen escapes his just tax, others must pay more. The maintenance of the system of voluntary self-assessment requires confidence in its fairness. Under the present system only a small proportion of the income tax returns filed each year can be adequately checked by the Internal Revenue Service. For this reason complete enforcement can hardly be expected. If each taxpayer approached the payment of his taxes as a contest in which the purpose was to outwit the adversary rather than as a civic duty, and if tax practitioners encouraged their clients to rationalize the rules to their own advantage, the system would be in danger of breakdown, as it has broken down in many other countries.

At the same time, it must be recognized that income for a short period, such as a year, and especially business income, is an elusive concept. There are wide areas in which subjective judgments must be exercised and this inevitably can lead to honest differences of opinion.

The Internal Revenue Service also is not without responsibility. If Revenue Agents approach examination of tax returns in a partisan spirit, with the objective of getting the most tax immediately by stretching the rules as far as possible in the government's favor; if they take advantage of technicalities inequitable to the taxpayer; if they insist on unnecessary adjustments of income or expenses between accounting periods; if Revenue Agents are rated for promotion on the basis of "production" of additional taxes—then taxpayers react defensively. They will view the government as an adversary, and come to regard the payment of taxes as a game, rather than a moral obligation.

In a message to IRS audit personnel, former Commissioner Caplin said that the attitude of the Service should be one of proper and reasonable appraisal of the merits of the issue. Decisions should not be issued by the potential tax adjustment involved. "We should never adopt a superior attitude; nor should we take advantage of the taxpayer's technical ignorance."

Certified public accountants practicing in the tax area have a sense of responsibility to the public, as well as to clients and the government. CPAs who earn the confidence of their clients and the Revenue Agents serve as a stabilizing force. They help greatly to maintain confidence in the country's tax system and to make it work with reasonable efficiency.

The CPA's responsibilities to his client, to the government, and to the public, though they have necessarily been discussed separately, are in fact interrelated. If the CPA properly serves the taxpayer, he is discharging his responsibility not only to his client but also to the government and to the public. If he keeps his client from overpaying his tax—and many taxpayers do overpay taxes—he is rendering an obvious and important service. If he does what he can to keep his client from underpaying his tax, he aids the government in the administration of the tax laws. He also serves the public, which otherwise would have a larger tax burden to bear.

Sec. 55 — STATEMENTS ON RESPONSIBILITIES
IN TAX PRACTICE

As the foregoing review suggests, there is a measure of agreement among CPAs about what the profession's responsibilities in tax practice are. The ethical problems involved have been given wide consideration. The Institute's committee on Federal taxation has learned that some standards of responsibility and practice already have wide acceptance among members of the American Institute. But they have not yet been widely communicated.

Now, for the first time, the profession is attempting in a series of statements issued by the Institute's committee on Federal taxation to articulate the CPA's responsibility to his client, the public, the government, and his profession.

The following are the principal objectives of the program:

1. To identify and develop appropriate standards of responsibilities in tax practice and to promote their uniform application by CPAs.
2. To encourage the development of increased understanding of the responsibilities of the CPA by the Internal Revenue Service.
3. To foster increased public integrity and confidence in the tax system, through awareness of self-imposed standards of conduct accepted by CPAs.
4. To protect CPAs against charges of misconduct resulting from misunderstanding regarding the extent of their responsibility.*

The announcement of the program makes it clear that the purpose of the statements is not to establish a separate code of conduct in tax practice apart from the general ethical precepts of the Institute's Code of Professional Ethics. They are intended simply as guides within the general tenets of the Code.**

The first two statements of the committee on Federal taxation are reprinted in the following sections.

Sec. 56 — THE FIRST STATEMENT — SIGNATURE OF PREPARER

I.   *Introduction.* Is it proper for a certified public accountant to prepare a Federal tax return and deliver it to the taxpayer without having signed the preparer's declaration?

II. *Statement.* A CPA should sign as preparer any Federal tax return which requires the signature of a preparer if he prepares it for and transmits it to the taxpayer or another, whether or not the return was prepared for compensation.

---

* "Statements on Responsibilities in Tax Practice: Introduction," issued by the committee on Federal taxation of the American Institute of CPAs, *The Journal of Accountancy*, October 1964, pages 65-66.
**Ibid., page 65.

III. *Explanation.* Section 1.6065-1(b)(1) of the Income Tax Regulations requires that a preparer must sign the preparer's declaration on a return providing for such verification where the return is prepared for a taxpayer for compensation or as an incident to the performance of other services for which compensation is received. It is clear that if the CPA is the "preparer" of a return (in the sense of the Regulation) he should sign the preparer's declaration and may not avoid doing so willfully. A CPA also should sign a return prepared by him whether or not it is prepared for compensation. Although this latter requirement goes beyond the scope of the Regulation, it represents a step in the establishment of uniform standards of responsibility in tax return preparation by CPAs.

A typical example of a preparer's declaration (taken from the 1963 Form 1040) follows:

> Under penalties of perjury, I declare that I have examined this return, including accompanying schedules and statements, and to the best of my knowledge and belief it is true, correct and complete. If prepared by a person other than taxpayer, his declaration is based on all information of which he has any knowledge.

The following examples reflect the committee's understanding of when the CPA is a "preparer." The examples are intended to be illustrative and are offered to provide a basis for resolving doubts which may arise in the course of a CPA's practice:

A. Situations considered to constitute the preparation of a return, and in which the CPA's signature as preparer is required.

   1. The CPA assembles information pertinent to the taxpayer's return, and completes the return and transmits it to the taxpayer. The CPA is required to sign the return as preparer whether the CPA prepares the return from information supplied by the taxpayer, or from information obtained by the CPA directly or indirectly from the

taxpayer's books and records. This requirement is unchanged whether the CPA conducted an examination of the financial statements in accordance with generally accepted auditing standards, or whether he expressed or disclaimed an opinion on them.

2. The CPA assembles information as in Situation A-1 above and completes a draft of the return but does not perform certain mechanical functions, such as typing or reproducing (e.g., the draft of the return is prepared in pencil), and forwards it to the taxpayer. The CPA's arrangement with the taxpayer should provide that before the return is filed, the taxpayer will make the draft and the return to be filed available to the CPA for proofing and signature.

3. The CPA prepares a return as in Situation A-1 above and transmits it to the taxpayer ready for filing, except for certain *minor* items or supplemental information which will not affect the taxable income or loss and which are to be inserted in the return by the taxpayer. The CPA should sign the return before it is transmitted to the taxpayer. An example of a minor item is a taxpayer's identification number; pension plan data is an example of supplemental information.

4. The CPA reviews a return originally prepared by the taxpayer or another and, under authority conferred by the taxpayer, either makes substantial changes in the return or substantial changes are made by the taxpayer or another at the CPA's direction. In this situation the CPA is considered to be a preparer, should sign the return and, accordingly, should satisfy himself as to the content of the entire return. On the other hand, if the CPA's engagement is limited to submitting recommendations, he is not considered to be a preparer. The term "substantial changes" means the revisions are significant in relation to the taxpayer's taxable income or loss, or the tax liability for the year. (Review situations in which the CPA is not the preparer will be discussed in a subsequent statement.)

B. Situations not considered to constitute the preparation of a return, and in which the CPA's signature as preparer is not required.

   1. A taxpayer transmits to a CPA an otherwise completed return with the request that the CPA perform certain mechanical service, such as typing or reproducing.

   2. In the course of an examination of financial statements the CPA assembles some, but not a preponderant part, of the information which is used for the preparation of a return by the client or another.

   3. The CPA prepares a schedule (e.g., capital gains, foreign tax credit, etc.) and transmits it to the taxpayer for inclusion in a return. The remainder of the return is completed by the taxpayer or another.

   4. In the course of an examination of financial statements: (a) The CPA makes a determination of taxable income or loss in considering the client's tax liability, but not in connection with the preparation of a return. (b) The CPA reviews a return prepared by the client or another, before it is filed, for the sole purpose of considering the client's tax liability. The CPA neither makes substantial changes (as described in Situation A-4) in the return nor are substantial changes made by the taxpayer or another at the CPA's direction.

   5. During or after the close of the taxable year the CPA advises a taxpayer as to the taxability, deductibility or presentation of certain items in a return.

(In each of the above situations it is assumed that the CPA did not perform additional services which, when taken together with the situation discussed, would constitute preparation of a return.)

C. Other situations.
   1. The CPA assembles information pertinent to the taxpayer's return, but discontinues work on it due to a disagreement with the taxpayer as to the presentation of an

item. At the taxpayer's request the CPA transmits to him the incomplete return. The CPA is not required to sign the incomplete return, and in his letter of transmittal should disavow responsibility as preparer.

2. The CPA prepared a return, signed and transmitted it to the taxpayer. The taxpayer requests that the CPA make certain changes. If the changes sought by the taxpayer meet with the approval of the CPA, the CPA should sign the return as revised. If the changes sought by the taxpayer are unacceptable to the CPA and an impasse develops, the CPA should refuse to revise the return or to sign a return as revised by the taxpayer.

In connection with an engagement to prepare a return, it should be recognized that the return, upon transmission to the taxpayer, belongs to the taxpayer. Before filing a return prepared by a CPA, a taxpayer could make changes in it without the CPA's knowledge or permission. It is recommended that the CPA preserve a copy of each return in the form in which it was transmitted to the taxpayer.

IV. *Applicability.* This statement is confined to Federal tax practice. It applies to the preparation of Federal tax returns by CPAs in public practice, and by CPAs in private employment to the extent that they prepare returns outside of their regular employment. The Regulations except employees from the requirement of verification of certain tax returns prepared by them, if prepared in the scope of their employment, for their employers or fellow employees. Therefore, they are excepted to that extent from the application of this statement.

Although, for convenience, this statement is written in terms of an individual CPA, it applies equally to the CPA's staff, members of a CPA partnership, and the staff of a CPA partnership.*

---

* "Statements on Responsibilities in Tax Practice No. 1: Signature of Preparer," issued by the committee on Federal taxation of the American Institute of CPAs, *The Journal of Accountancy,* October 1964, pages 66-67.

NOTE

This statement has been approved by at least two-thirds of the members of the committee on Federal taxation, reached on a formal vote after examination of the subject matter. It has not been considered and acted upon by the Council of the Institute. Its authority rests upon the statutes and regulations of the taxing authority and the general acceptability of the committee's interpretations. The statement is not intended to be retroactive.

Sec. 57 — THE SECOND STATEMENT — SIGNATURE OF REVIEWER: ASSUMPTION OF PREPARER'S RESPONSIBILITY

I. *Introduction.* Frequently, a certified public accountant is engaged to review a Federal tax return by a taxpayer who seeks added assurance that it has been prepared properly. In many such instances, the taxpayer requests that the CPA sign or cosign the preparer's declaration on the return.

   This statement considers whether a CPA who is not the preparer of a return, and therefore is not required to sign the preparer's declaration, nevertheless in his discretion may sign and thus assume the preparer's responsibility.

   Statement No. 1 issued in September 1964 discusses the signature requirement for a CPA who is the preparer of a Federal tax return.

II. *Statement.* If the CPA is not the preparer of a Federal tax return, he is not required to sign the preparer's declaration. However, in his discretion, the CPA may sign the declaration on a return prepared by the taxpayer or another if he reviews the return and, in the course of the review, acquires knowledge with respect to the return substantially equivalent to that which he would have acquired had he prepared the return. Unless such review is made, the CPA should not sign the preparer's declaration.

III. *Explanation.*

   A. General. This statement is concerned with situations

in which the CPA's role is that of a reviewer with no obligation to sign as preparer. Statement No. 1 provides examples and discussion relating to whether in certain situations the CPA is the preparer of a Federal tax return. It also covers one type of situation in which a review becomes tantamount to preparation and the CPA should sign as preparer (Statement No. 1, Part III A-4).

The Internal Revenue Code, the Income Tax Regulations (including Section 1.6065-1(b)(1)) and tax return forms make no reference to the signing by a reviewer of the preparer's declaration. Thus, it appears that the CPA who signs the preparer's declaration assumes the same responsibility whether he is a preparer or a reviewer. Accordingly, unless the CPA-reviewer intends to assume the same responsibility as a preparer for the entire return, he should not sign the preparer's declaration.

A CPA who has reviewed a return (prepared by the taxpayer or another) to the extent set forth in the following paragraph may sign the preparer's declaration. However, he is not required to sign unless he is considered to have become the preparer in circumstances such as those described in Statement No. 1.

Before a CPA-reviewer signs the preparer's declaration on a return prepared by a taxpayer or another, he should acquire knowledge with respect to the return substantially equivalent to that which he would have acquired had he prepared the return. It is contemplated that review procedures will vary from return to return and that the CPA will apply his professional judgment in each engagement to determine the extent of the review needed to acquire such knowledge.

B. *Cosigning.* Where a return has been prepared for a taxpayer by a person who signed as preparer and a CPA is asked to review and cosign the return, the CPA may add his signature to the preparer's declaration provided that his review meets the standard set forth in the preceding paragraph.

IV. *Applicability*. This statement is confined to Federal tax practice. It applies to the review of Federal tax returns by CPAs in public practice and by CPAs in private employment to the extent that they practice outside of their regular employment.

Although, for convenience, this statement is written in terms of an individual CPA, it applies equally to the CPA's staff, members of a CPA partnership, and the staff of a CPA partnership.*

Sec. 58 — THE FUTURE OF THE PROGRAM

The chairman of the subcommittee of the Federal taxation committee charged with the responsibility of drafting statements on responsibilities has said that the selection of a non-controversial topic for the first statement was deliberate. "Priority has been given," he writes, "to the simpler topics concerning tax return preparation with the intention of working up to the more troublesome subjects at a later time." He adds that the mere issuance of a few statements will have a salutary effect on tax practice as a whole. He thinks that this will prove to be a conditioning factor in developing acceptance for the more controversial items to follow.**

The next two or three statements will deal with some aspect of tax return preparation. Other topics under consideration include the following: Answers to Questions on Returns; Com-

---

*"Statements on Responsibilities in Tax Practice No. 2, Signature of Reviewer: Assumption of Preparer's Responsibility," issued by the committee on Federal taxation of the American Institute of CPAs, *The Journal of Accountancy*, September 1965, pages 62-63. This statement was followed by a note identical to that which followed the first statement.

**Matthew F. Blake, "Statements of Responsibilities in Tax Practice," *The Journal of Accountancy*, April 1964, pages 37-41.

pliance with Administrative Determination of a Prior Year; Knowledge of Client's Noncompliance; Error or Omission.

This program, which represents the first attempt by anyone to outline the responsibilities of tax practitioners, merits the acclaim of tax practitioners, the Internal Revenue Service and all taxpayers.

Sec. 59 — ETHICAL RESPONSIBILITIES INVOLVED IN
RELATIONS WITH THE LEGAL PROFESSION
IN TAX PRACTICE

In all phases of tax practice, questions of accounting and questions of law may arise.

It is generally conceded by authoritative spokesmen of both professions that lawyers and CPAs have an ethical responsibility to safeguard the interests of their clients by refraining from giving service or advice which requires the training and skill of a member of the other profession.

This proposition is in harmony with the general ethical responsibility of a member of any recognized profession not to give service or advice which he is not competent to give. (See Chapter 2.)

The difficulty of applying the general proposition in practice is rooted in the difficulty of defining what constitutes a "question of law" and a "question of accounting" in a particular tax matter. Neither term has been generally defined by accepted authority, and there is doubt that either ever can be.

In an interpretation of Circular No. 230, issued by the Secretary of the Treasury on January 30, 1956, it is made clear that enrolled agents and attorneys are responsible for determining when the assistance of a member of the other profession is required. Both are expected to respect the appropriate fields of each.*

---

*See *The Journal of Accountancy,* March 1956, page 6, and the interpretive opinion of the Institute's counsel, *The Journal of Accountancy,* April 1956, page 30.

Thus, the Treasury Department has adopted the ethical principle that a practitioner should not venture beyond the bounds of his professional competence. This ethical responsibility had previously been imposed on members of the two professions by their national organizations. It was in 1951 that the House of Delegates of the American Bar Association and the Council of the American Institute approved a "Statement of Principles Relating to Practice in the Field of Federal Income Taxation Promulgated by the National Conference of Lawyers and Certified Public Accountants." This statement, like other utterances on the subject, does not provide definitions of "questions of law," or "questions of accounting." For the most part, it consists of admonitions to members of the two professions not to venture beyond the fields of their respective professional competence.*

Operating under this statement the National Conference of Lawyers and Certified Public Accountants has been instrumental in avoiding controversy between the two professions. This work has been supplemented at the state level by conferences and cooperating committees of CPAs and lawyers which are now in existence in forty states.

Certified public accountants in tax practice, as in other types of work, are responsible for determining when the limits of their own professional competence require that a lawyer should be consulted. This principle applies not only to lawyers but to other professional experts or technicians whose knowledge and skills may be useful to the client. In tax matters, for example, questions arise not infrequently in which the advice and assistance of engineers, appraisers, economists, statisticians, and other experts would be helpful. The CPA handling the engagement should not attempt to deal with questions of this kind which he is not equipped to answer but should see to it that a professionally competent technician is consulted. Only thus can the best interests of the client be served.

*For the full text see *The Journal of Accountancy,* April 1956, pages 32-33.

Sec. 60 — EMPLOYMENT OF LAWYERS BY CERTIFIED
PUBLIC ACCOUNTANTS

Certified public accountants practicing individually and in
partnership have on occasion employed, as members of their
staffs, persons who have been admitted to the bar. Members
of the legal profession have questioned this practice on the
ground that it signified an intention to "practice law." It is
illegal for a nonlawyer to employ a lawyer on a salary and
through him to perform legal services for the public.

Accounting firms have pointed out that their staff employees
who have had a legal education were engaged and trained
as accountants, that they performed accounting rather than
legal services, and that their activities were restricted to those
which their employer was permitted to perform.

The National Conference of Lawyers and CPAs has agreed
that lawyers employed by accounting firms and CPAs employed by law firms should not be permitted to do anything
which their employers are not authorized to do.

This principle is embodied in Rule 4.03 of the Institute's
Code of Professional Ethics. (See Chapter 2, pages 15-16.)

Sec. 61 — JOINT PRACTICE OF ACCOUNTING
AND LAW

Bar Associations, with some exceptions, have generally held it
to be unethical for lawyers to form partnerships with CPAs to
engage in the joint practice of law and accounting.

In Opinion 239 (February 21, 1942) the American Bar Association committee on ethics held that a partnership between
a lawyer and a CPA to act as consultants in Federal tax matters
and to represent taxpayers before the Treasury Department
was improper.

Opinion No. 269 (June 21, 1945) of the same committee
states in effect that a partnership between a lawyer and an

accountant to specialize in income tax work is permissible only if the lawyer ceases to hold himself out as such and confines his activities to those that are open to accountants.

In Opinion No. 297 (February 24, 1961) the American Bar Association committee ruled that a lawyer who was also a CPA could not hold himself out to the public as qualified in both professions but must decide whether to practice as a lawyer or a CPA.

The professional accounting societies have not promulgated any rules on this subject. Nothing in the American Institute's Code of Professional Ethics or in its numbered opinions would prevent an Institute member who was also a lawyer from holding himself out as qualified to practice both professions. Likewise, nothing would prevent an Institute member from forming a partnership with a lawyer whose principal occupation was tax work. If the lawyer performed other types of legal services outside the practice of public accounting, the CPA could not share fees with him because of Rule 3.04. (See Chapter 8, pages 137-138.)

Not all questions about the joint practice of law and public accounting have been resolved and the entire field will have continuing consideration in the future.

Chapter 7

ETHICAL RESPONSIBILITIES
IN MANAGEMENT SERVICES

IN THE broadest sense, the term "management services" includes all services rendered by certified public accountants. The audit of financial statements and the expression of opinions on them provide information and assurance which are useful to management, although the primary objective may be to report to stockholders or credit grantors. Even if exclusively intended for the latter purpose, audits serve management in facilitating the acquisition of needed capital. Tax work is certainly a service to management.

But the term "management services" is usually applied in a narrower sense to any services rendered by CPAs other than auditing and tax work. CPAs have always rendered some services of this description, but often as a casual and unplanned outgrowth of the auditing and tax work which constitute the bulk of the practice of most certified public accountants.

For this reason some CPAs have not consciously equipped themselves to render a broad range of management services, and therefore do not offer such services as a regular and important part of their practices. The field itself is in a process of evolution and the pace of this evolution is accelerating. As a result there is a wide diversity in the extent to which CPA firms have extended their services in this area of practice.

Sec. 62 — WIDENING DEMAND FOR MANAGEMENT SERVICES

There is a mounting demand from business enterprises, governmental units and nonprofit institutions for expert aid in all phases of management which will increase efficiency and minimize costs. This demand comes from organizations both large and small. It springs from the increasing complexity of our economic system and the increasing intensity of competition in an era of rapid technological improvements. No one man can be technically competent to deal with all the management problems of modern business. Businessmen require help in planning, control and decision making. A manager's intuitive judgment alone is no longer adequate. Facts, figures, and a systematic approach to the solution of business problems are now generally recognized as essential to survival.

Certified public accountants are well equipped by their technical training and professional experience to help management in the processes of planning, control and decision making. By virtue of their familiarity with their clients' organizations, acquired through auditing and tax work, CPAs are in a position to undertake many management services, within the limits of their professional competence, without the orientation in the affairs of a business which would be necessary if an outside expert, unfamiliar with the organization, were brought in for this purpose. They can also correlate specific problems with the over-all financial structure of the business.

It is generally agreed that CPAs may need to undertake additional study and research, and in some areas to undergo special training, in order to perform types of services to management which they have not rendered in the past. In many areas adequate skill and knowledge can be acquired readily by one who already has a sound foundation in auditing, accounting theory and practice, and taxation. Other management services are more highly specialized and require intensive training.

Sec. 63 — SCOPE OF CPAS' MANAGEMENT SERVICES

How far should certified public accountants go in expanding the scope of their management services?

In April 1961 the Institute's Council gave a definitive answer to this question by adopting the following resolution:

> It is an objective of the Institute, recognizing that management service activities are a proper function of CPAs, to encourage all CPAs to perform the entire range of management services consistent with their professional competence, ethical standards, and responsibility.

Many CPAs believe that they have a duty to offer management services to their clients. They feel that clients who engage CPAs as auditors and tax advisors are entitled to expect expert services in any area of accounting and finance in which management has problems.*

One way to broaden the scope of service is to build gradually from within. One or more partners may be assigned to the task of studying the field of management services and of training staff to perform the services which the firm decides to undertake.**

---

* See, for example, Norman J. Lenhart and Philip Defliese, *Montgomery's Auditing*, Eighth Edition, Ronald Press Company, New York, 1957, page 539.
**Roger Wellington, "The Development of Management Services," *The Journal of Accountancy,* June 1956, pages 57-59.

Another approach is to employ specialists who are already expert in various areas of management services — such as budgeting, cost accounting, inventory control and operations research as staff assistants of the existing firm. If this method is employed, one or more partners of the firm should be competent to supervise and evaluate the work of such specialists.

It has been suggested that proficiency in this area of practice may be built in the following ways: (1) working under experienced supervision, (2) taking on simple problems before complex ones, (3) reading and study, (4) taking courses offered by colleges and professional societies, (5) researching for solutions to problems during the course of engagements.

Sec. 64 — WHAT ARE MANAGEMENT SERVICES?

Difficulty in discussing the field of management services arises from the absence of an authoritative definition. The term means different things to different people. The uncertainties as to what is being talked about complicate the ethical considerations that must enter into any discussion of the subject.

Some CPAs would limit management services to "all of those consulting and advisory activities in which the CPA is expert because of his understanding of: (1) the traditional accounting and financial processes of business organizations, and (2) the related information and control systems used by management in accomplishing its business objectives."

The following have been cited as examples of such services: considering inventory valuation policies, discussing depreciation procedures, establishing rules for the expensing of repairs and maintenance; advising on investment problems, credit policies, cash management, stockholder relations, development of cost systems, conversion of manual accounting procedures to machine procedures, design of internal financial statements, design of inventory and production control methods; consulting on record-keeping problems of personnel systems, and advice on other special-purpose information systems in fields such as marketing and sales.

However, many CPAs involved in management services have taken a different position. Since the range of subject matter of management services is so extensive as to appear infinite, they believe that no definition of management services can result from an itemization of subject matter to be mastered. Rather, it is contended, the rendering of such services involves a combination of professional skills and technical procedures applied to a wide variety of management problems. Subject matter is mastered along the way. The CPA helps his client to higher profits through application of a problem-solving approach to the client's affairs.

These and other differing definitions, while not necessarily mutually exclusive, demonstrate that the profession has not yet reached agreement on the precise nature of management services which CPAs may properly render. Perhaps it will never be possible to develop an all-inclusive definition.

However, there is general agreement that the natural point of departure for CPAs who wish to expand the scope of their services to management is the clients' information system, with which CPAs are already familiar as auditors. The improvement and effective utilization of the information system, as a tool to help management run its business better, offer broad enough scope to absorb the energies of most small CPA firms for many years to come. Meanwhile, there is no immediate need to place arbitrary limitations on the scope of services which larger firms may equip themselves to render. Experience and economic forces may produce answers to the question of optimum scope in another decade or two.

Discussion of ethical problems in the field of management services, however, is complicated at present by the imprecision of the term and the rapid diversification of the types of work which are so described. It is possible only to point out questions that have arisen, and to indicate varying points of view which have been expressed. Few of the statements which follow can be considered authoritative.

The ethical questions which arise in relation to management services by CPAs bring into sharp focus the basic concepts underlying the code of ethics of the accounting profession. It is therefore recommended that in considering the problems discussed in this chapter, the reader refer also to Chapters 2, 3 and 4 of this book.

Sec. 65 — COMPETENCE

The growing demand for management services, and the increasing number of speeches and articles encouraging certified public accountants to turn their attention to this field, may lead many CPAs to assume that they are qualified to perform management services which are in fact beyond their competence. Nothing would discredit the accounting profession more rapidly than a general tendency on the part of CPAs to undertake engagements for which they are not qualified. Loss of clients' confidence would have adverse effects even on the more familiar areas of accounting practice.

Are CPAs competent to render management services? The answer to this question is a qualified yes. Because of the pervasive nature of accounting, the academic training and the examination requirement for the CPA certificate provide a broad base on which to build a management services practice.

Nevertheless, the fact that a man is a CPA does not automatically qualify him to render the entire range of management services. The ethical and legal requirement of competence must still be met. In fact, since the subject matter of management services is so extensive that no one person could develop specialized knowledge in all areas, the full range of management services (whatever that may prove to be) should be performed only by a firm which includes both generalists and specialists.

In determining whether in fairness to his client he is in a position to undertake a given management services engagement, the CPA should consider his own background and ability as objectively as possible. He may not begin with complete knowledge of the characteristics of the business in question or of the available techniques; but he must either acquire the necessary knowledge or decline to serve and refer the engagement to someone else.

Sec. 66 — SPECIALIZATION, CONSULTATION
AND REFERRAL

When his client needs management services which the CPA is not competent to render, the CPA should recommend consultation with, or referral of the engagement to, another CPA, an engineer or other specialist. Such a recommendation is in itself a useful service, and the CPA will often find it possible to participate in the engagement by working with the specialist. In coordinating his services with others, a CPA should, in any reports or recommendations rendered, make clear the limitations of responsibilities assumed and services rendered.

It should be noted that these restrictions do not preclude a CPA from hiring specialists for advice and assistance in other matters. For example, he may need the services of an expert in appraising inventories of precious jewels. "To determine the correctness of the reserves for losses of an insurance company, he may need the services of an actuary. Or he may need a lawyer to interpret a contract. But in these and similar cases, the work of the specialist is for the accountant and not for the client."*

*Ira N. Frisbee, "Ethical Considerations in Rendering Management Services," *The Journal of Accountancy*, March 1957, page 33.

In medicine and law, specialization has developed to a marked extent, and there are signs that it is widening rapidly in the accounting profession. As the profession extends its activities farther into the field of management services, individuals and firms will of necessity specialize to a greater degree.

Up to now, certified public accountants have shown a reluctance to refer their clients' problems to specialists within their own profession. While the reasons for this attitude are understandable, it may, if it persists, retard the potential development of the profession as a whole.

If CPAs are unwilling to call in fellow practitioners to help with problems requiring specialized knowledge, the clients may be forced to go outside the accounting profession for assistance which CPA specialists may be as well qualified, or in some cases, better qualified, to give. Even worse, the client may be shut off from needed service available from within the accounting profession, by the reluctance of their CPAs to point out problems which could be solved only with the collaboration of a specialist.

The need for referral service is more acute in management services than it is in auditing and taxes. In general, CPAs have kept abreast of developments in the two latter fields, but the expansion of management services has resulted in a situation in which some firms offer the specialized services and others do not. The existence of this disparity creates a need for consultations and referrals.*

The fear that the consultant might take over the regular accounting work formerly performed by the CPA who called him in resulted in the adoption of Rule 5.02, which reads as follows:

> A member or associate who receives an engagement for services by referral from another member or associate shall not

*Henry DeVos, Ed., *Management Services Handbook*, published by the American Institute of Certified Public Accountants, New York, 1964, page 60.

discuss or accept an extension of his services beyond the specific engagement without first consulting with the referring member or associate.

It may be possible to provide a referral service that would protect the interests of both parties if an *elective* rather than a *mandatory* code of assurances could be established.* (See Chapter 2, Sections 9-11.)

Sec. 67 — INDEPENDENCE

The question of whether a CPA's independence as auditor is jeopardized by the rendering of management services for the same client has been discussed at length in Chapter 3, pages 21-28. The following paragraph from Opinion No. 12 summarizes the ethics committee's view of the matter:

> The committee does not intend to suggest . . . that the rendering of professional services other than the independent audit itself would suggest to a reasonable observer a conflict of interest. For example, in the areas of management advisory services and tax practice, so long as the CPA's services consist of advice and technical assistance, the committee can discern no likelihood of a conflict of interest arising from such services. It is a rare instance for management to surrender its responsibility to make management decisions. However, should a member make such decisions on matters affecting the company's financial position or results of operations, it would appear that his objectivity as independent auditor of the company's financial statements might well be impaired. Consequently, such situations should be avoided.

Since third party interest is not involved in the rendering of services to management, the standards of audit-independence need not be applied when the CPA renders manage-

Ibid., page 61.

ment assistance to a nonaudit client.* Nevertheless, in such a situation a member and his staff should maintain a general independence of attitude. They should be objective, unbiased and forthright in dealings with the client's management.

Sec. 68 — THE PROFESSIONAL ATTITUDE

Because management services are a new field for many CPAs, those who equip themselves to render such services have a natural impulse to inform their clients that the extended services are available. There is no ethical objection to the transmittal of such information to clients by personal letter or by word of mouth.

Many CPA firms, however, have attempted to accelerate the dissemination of such information to clients by the preparation of brochures outlining the services offered. Others have prepared monographs on techniques of managerial accounting which, published under the firm name, suggest that the firm is available to render services in the area of management activity described. Other firms have produced slide films or motion pictures directed to the same end, and designed to be exhibited to personnel of client organizations.

In general, a CPA may send his clients any information which he believes would interest them (see Chapter 4, page 51). This material may serve a useful purpose in keeping clients informed, but its distribution should be restricted to staff members, clients, lawyers of clients, bankers and others with whom professional contacts are maintained. The committee has held that copies of such material may also be given to nonclients who specifically request them. The member who grants requests for multiple copies of such publications must assume responsibility for any additional distribution they may receive. (See Opinion 9, page 197.)

*James E. Redfield, A *Study of Management Services by CPAs*, The University of Texas, Austin, 1961, page 33.

Sec. 69 — CORPORATIONS FORMED TO RENDER
MANAGEMENT SERVICES

It has been asked whether some of the partners of a CPA firm may become officers or stockholders of a separate corporation, of which engineers or other specialists would also be officers and stockholders, which would offer management services exclusively, while the accounting firm continued to offer the customary accounting, auditing and tax services.

Rule 4.06 of the Institute's Code of Professional Ethics forbids members to practice public accounting in corporate form. It reads as follows:

> A member or associate shall not be an officer, director, stockholder, representative, or agent of any corporation engaged in the practice of public accounting in any state or territory of the United States or the District of Columbia.

Rule 4.05 requires Institute members engaged in rendering "services of a type performed by public accountants" to observe all the provisions of the Code of Professional Ethics.

Taken together, these two rules have been construed to mean that if the proposed corporation renders services of a type performed by public accountants, an Institute member may not become an officer, director, stockholder, representative or agent of the corporation.

Sec. 70 — SEPARATE PARTNERSHIPS FOR
MANAGEMENT SERVICES

If instead of forming a separate corporation some of the partners of a CPA firm formed a separate partnership with engineers or other specialists, would this be a violation?

Rule 4.06, prohibiting corporate practice would not be involved. A separate partnership of management consultants, which rendered "services of a type performed by public accountants" could not advertise or solicit engagements without exposing the CPA-partners to a charge of violation of Rule 4.05. Such a partnership would undoubtedly be precluded by law from holding itself out to the public as a firm of certified public accountants, since some of its members would be non-CPAs. Moreover, because of the prohibition against the designation of specialties (see Opinion No. 11), the partnership could not hold itself out as "management consultants" or otherwise indicate the nature of the services offered without exposing the CPA-partners to charges of violating the Institute's prohibition against the advertising of professional attainments or services.

Despite these restrictions many such "mixed partnerships" have been formed. The principal reason for forming such a partnership is to enable trained specialists who are not CPAs to receive recognition and partnership status and to share in the profits of the firm. An arrangement of this kind may result from an agreement between a professional accounting firm and a partnership of, let us say, operations research specialists. Some partners of the accounting firm, without giving up their status as members of the CPA partnership, may form a separate partnership with the operations research men. The newly formed firm may have a personal name combining elements of the titles of the accounting firm and of the original operations research firm. This results in (1) an all-CPA accounting firm holding itself out as CPAs and performing accounting, auditing, tax and management services; and (2) a "mixed partnership" of CPAs and management specialists, not indicating the services it is prepared to perform, but rendering certain specialized management services.

Questions have been raised about the propriety of such arrangements.

First, is there a violation of the accountancy law of a regulatory state when CPAs form a partnership with unlicensed persons? The answer seems to depend on whether or not the services to be rendered are regulated under law. If the accountancy law reserves only the attest function to those licensed, then unlicensed persons may freely perform all other accounting services, including specialized management and consulting work. If the state board contends that the CPA members of the separate partnership are in violation of the ethical rule prohibiting the sharing of the fees of professional work with nonpractitioners, the specialized partnership might argue that, as far as the law is concerned, it is not engaged in work that can be regulated by the state, since it does not express professional opinions resulting from an audit.

Second, would the CPA partners of such a "mixed partnership" be in violation of the Institute's rule prohibiting the sharing of fees with nonpractitioners?

If it is held that the operations research men are essentially laymen with whom CPAs may not share fees under Rule 3.04, then the firm in question may argue that if the services rendered are held to be those of a type performed by public accountants (Rule 4.05) the specialists are not laymen but specialized accounting practitioners with whom CPAs may properly share fees. On the other hand, if the services are not of a type performed by public accountants, it may be argued that Rule 3.04 is not applicable, since the "fees" referred to therein must be assumed to be fees derived from professional accounting services.

The committee on professional ethics has therefore expressed the opinion that:

> ... nothing in the Institute's Code of Professional Ethics presently prohibits a member from forming, or becoming a member of, a separate partnership with non-CPA specialists for the rendering of various management services as long as such partnership observes the by-laws and Code of Professional

Ethics. Such a separate partnership would not be permitted to advertise, solicit clients, accept commissions, or do anything else prohibited by the Code. Nor would it be permitted to hold itself out on letterheads, cards, signs, etc., in directory listings or through its partnership name as specializing in a particular service.*

Apart from the rule against fee-splitting, which was probably adopted with entirely different circumstances in mind, other interesting questions arise with regard to the potentialities of mixed partnerships.

For example, nothing would prevent a CPA firm from "acquiring" a partnership of non-CPA specialists. At present, partnerships acquired by CPA firms include specialists in actuarial services, pension and profit-sharing plans, and operations research. Accounting firms of the future may acquire many other types of service organizations by establishing multiple partnerships which could render services to their clients in almost any field not prohibited by law.

It is, of course, possible for a CPA firm today, to perform any and all services not prohibited by law, through employment of specialists on its staff—assuming CPA partners of the firm are competent to evaluate and supervise such services. Whether the extension of services through mixed partnerships—in which CPA partners assume full responsibility for compliance with the Code of Ethics—is inimical in any way to the public interest, or raises any new ethical questions, has not yet been authoritatively determined.

Carried to extremes, proliferation of services may tend to obscure the identity of CPAs as professional masters of a specific body of knowledge. Perhaps there is need for a conceptual description of what constitutes the professional practice of accounting, which could help to answer some of the questions which have been raised. The forthcoming study of the "Common Body of Knowledge of CPAs" may furnish a clue.

*Opinion No. 17, page 211.

When a firm of specialists is "acquired" by a CPA firm through creation of a mixed partnership, the clientele of the specialist firm may be acquired along with it.

Many of these clients of the specialist firm may already be served by other public accountants. It must be assumed that the CPA firm cannot consider such clients to be clients of its own.

Any other assumption would obscure the meaning of "client." The ethics committee has taken the position that a CPA may properly inform his clients of the various services he is prepared to offer. This is not considered solicitation. But it would hardly make sense to hold that one business could be the client of a half-dozen CPA firms simultaneously, each rendering different services through mixed specialist-partnerships, and each vying with the others to expand the scope of the services it rendered.

The committee on professional ethics currently has these important problems under study. The questions which have arisen doubtless stem from the fact that the Code of Professional Ethics refers to "services of a type performed by public accountants" but does not specify what these services are, or even describe their general nature. As a widening range of management services is added to the traditional accounting functions, and there is no definition of management services by CPAs, then the definition of public accounting itself becomes "open-end" and the extent of the services unlimited. Logical and semantic difficulties in applying existing rules of ethics are to be expected.

Sec. 71 — INCOMPATIBLE OCCUPATIONS

Rule 4.04 of the Institute's Code of Professional Ethics reads as follows:

> A member or associate shall not engage in any business or occupation conjointly with that of a public accountant, which is incompatible or inconsistent therewith.

If a practicing CPA also participated in a corporation which rendered management services of a type *not* performed by public accountants, it is possible that Rule 4.06, forbidding the practice of public accounting in corporate form, would not apply. However, such participation might be held incompatible with the practice of public accounting on the ground that the corporation would serve as a "feeder" to the accounting practice. The corporation would naturally refer to the "affiliated" accounting firm any clients who needed accounting, auditing or tax services. If the corporation advertised its services or solicited business, reference of clients by the corporation to the accounting firm would probably be regarded as indirect evasion of the rules against advertising and solicitation as they apply to the accounting firm.

The Institute's committee on professional ethics has stated that it has no desire to restrict unduly business or investment activities in which members may engage outside of their professional practices. There is no reason why a practicing CPA should not own stock, even a controlling interest, in a corporation engaged in manufacturing, for example, which has no evident relationship to the CPA's activities in the practice of his profession. (Obviously he could not serve as auditor of such a corporation.) However, the committee believes that some outside activities or investments might impair the certified public accountant's independence, or might result in situations in which division of fees with the laity would occur, or in which the rules against advertising and solicitation might be infringed, or might reflect adversely on the dignity of the profession. Such activities would be held "incompatible" under Rule 4.04.

The committee has never issued a list of occupations considered to be incompatible with public accounting. The reason for this is that a decision must depend upon the precise circumstances in each case. In general, the committee tries to dissuade members from engaging in secondary occupations which may involve a prospective client's financial affairs. On this basis the committee has discouraged members from taking out an insurance broker's license or from affiliating with an insurance agency. There are similar dangers in a practicing CPA's engaging in brokerage or real estate activities. If a practicing CPA decided to add to his professional income by serving as a mutual fund salesman, it is likely that he would become involved in discussions of prospective customers' personal finances which would tempt him to offer his services as a CPA in handling tax or accounting problems. This would violate the rule against solicitation but, perhaps more importantly, would reflect adversely on the dignity of the profession.

Sec. 72 — NON-CPAS AS PARTNERS OF ACCOUNTING FIRMS

Can non-CPA management experts be made partners of a CPA firm?

Rule 3.04 would prevent a member from sharing fees with, and consequently from forming a partnership with, a nonpractitioner. But if the management expert, as a principal occupation, rendered services of a type performed by public accountants—which services of course include management services—then he would be regarded as a practitioner and Rule 3.04 would not apply. However, all the other rules, including the prohibition against the indication of specialties, would apply and the CPA member of the firm would be held accountable for any ethical violations on the part of the management expert.

Not only would such a "mixed partnership" be prevented from holding itself out as "management consultants," but it would also be prohibited under the laws of most states from holding itself out as CPAs, since the management expert partner is not certified. Further, such a partnership would not be permitted to express opinions on financial statements if this activity is restricted, under state law, to CPAs and licensed public accountants.

The ethics committee expects that ultimately practicing CPAs will not enter into partnerships with anyone except other CPAs. However, the problems of drafting a rule of conduct that would effectively prohibit mixed partnerships are considerable. Presumably there would be no intention of preventing members from forming partnerships with laymen to carry on businesses or occupations not incompatible with the practice of public accounting. This means that the rule would have to state in effect that a member could not form a partnership with a non-CPA for the purpose of practicing public accounting. This would again raise the question of the exact limits of the practice of public accounting.

Sec. 73 — EMPLOYMENT OF EXPERTS AS
STAFF ASSISTANTS

Is it proper for a CPA firm to employ engineers, or other specialists, as members of the staff?

There is no rule against it, and no basis for objection on ethical grounds if such specialists are employed in work which the firm is permitted to undertake as part of the practice of accounting. Nevertheless, it is probably neither wise nor appropriate for a CPA firm to assume professional responsibility for services of a specialized nature rendered by its employees, unless at least one of the partners of the firm is competent to evaluate and supervise such services.

This requirement of supervisory competence has not yet been officially adopted, but common sense—and possibly the common law—support its wisdom. It goes beyond Rule 4.03, which states in effect that a member shall not permit an employee to perform for a client services which the member or his firm is not *permitted* to perform—permitted, presumably, by law.

Sec. 74 — ELECTRONIC DATA PROCESSING SERVICES

Many CPAs working in the field of management services have specialized not in subject matter but in techniques. One important technique is the elimination of clerical operations by the use of business machines. Machine accounting has logically evolved into electronic data processing which in turn has become part of the current computer revolution.

Computer technology is important to CPAs not only because of its impact on the accounting systems of their clients, but because of its influence on CPAs' own practices. Others are interested in this new field—others who do not operate under the ethical restrictions imposed on professional men. They may therefore treat the processing of accounting data like any other business. Since the machines involved are expensive and at present have a high obsolescence factor, substantial capital outlays are required even to obtain the equipment. Service centers may raise the necessary funds, and incidentally avoid individual liability, by incorporating their businesses. The speeds with which computers can process data are so great that promotional methods are adopted in order to keep them running at capacity. The service centers therefore advertise and solicit freely.

As a result, certified public accountants from all parts of the country report that their clients are being solicited by service centers offering to take over various accounting functions, including the preparation of balance sheets and income statements. More recently, state and national banks, many of which have computerized their own internal operations, utilize the idle time on this machinery to process accounting data for their depositors and others. Such services may be widely advertised.

Computers can now process tax data, make all the computations and print individual, and even corporate, tax returns. In addition, they can perform many management services, including cost and distribution analysis, aging of receivables, budget comparisons, and inventory control.

CPAs who have developed practices largely consisting of bookkeeping, write-up work and tax-return preparation are clearly threatened by these developments. But the potential capacities of computers are so great that it is impossible to predict their ultimate impact on business information systems, on the entire spectrum of management planning, control and decision-making, and even on the independent audit of financial statements.

However, certain ethical aspects of this revolutionary movement may appropriately be discussed here.

Relying on the maxim "If you can't lick 'em, join 'em," many CPAs have themselves decided to provide mechanical or electronic statistical or data processing services to small or medium-sized businesses. There is no ethical impropriety in this. In fact, in some ways it represents only a speeding up of the write-up services which CPAs have rendered for many years. But the ethics committee has held (Opinion No. 7, page 195) that members may render such services to the public, either as part of their regular accounting practices or in separate partnerships with others, only if they abide by all the provisions of the Code of Professional Ethics, notably those rules forbidding advertising, solicitation and practice in corporate form. Furthermore, Opinion No. 11, interpreting the advertising rule, precludes a member who offers these services from holding himself out as a specialist in data processing.

The proscription against indicating specialties would limit him to holding himself out as a certified public accountant.

In view of the computer challenge, perhaps this position should at least be re-examined. It rests on Rule 4.05, which requires a member to abide by the provisions of the Code when he renders "services of the type performed by public accountants." But computerized accounting services are now widely performed by lay corporations. If CPAs cannot compete, they may in effect abdicate the entire field of internal accounting for small business. The ultimate consequences, in terms of opportunities for professional management services, tax advice, and access to new clients by young CPAs commencing practice, are difficult to predict.

Yet, if CPAs are to compete by offering computerized accounting services themselves, it may be necessary to permit them to announce that they are equipped to do so—as the service centers and banks so widely advertise.

There are obvious dangers in permitting advertising of any services which CPAs perform. Where will the line be drawn? But the profession is confronted by a new situation which could not have been foreseen at the time the present rules were drafted. At the least, it deserves serious and prompt reconsideration.

Of course, CPAs are free to offer EDP services to their own clients. Some firms do this, but the volume must be large in order for the operation to be financially successful. Other certified public accountants have met this problem in local areas by forming an all-CPA computer center to offer these services to other CPA firms in the area. By this means they have been able to raise enough capital to purchase the necessary equipment and to have a large enough market to keep the machines operating economically—and without advertising or solicitation. Such CPA computer centers usually do not offer their services to the public, except through the medium of other CPAs.

Under the existing ethics rules and committee interpretations, this method of performing EDP services seems to offer Institute members the best opportunity to serve their clients in this challenging field.

Sec. 75 — ADVANTAGE OF ETHICAL STANDARDS IN MANAGEMENT SERVICES

When a certified public accountant undertakes to render management services, he makes them part of his public accounting practice, and in performing them he is subject to all the provisions of the Code of Professional Ethics, just as he is in other phases of his work.

Because management services are a comparatively new field to many CPAs, questions frequently arise as to the application of existing ethical rules to unfamiliar situations which occur in the management area. Such questions, for example, relate to contingent fees (Rule 1.04), forecasts (Rule 2.04), advertising (Rule 3.01), solicitation (Rule 3.02), division of fees with nonpractitioners (Rule 3.04), use of a CPA's name by another (Rule 4.02), employment of specialists (Rule 4.03), incompatible occupations (Rule 4.04), encroachment (Rule 5.01), and referrals (Rule 5.02).

In fact, the committee on professional ethics has said that "all the provisions of the Code of Professional Ethics apply to management advisory services, except those rules solely applicable to the expression of an opinion on financial statements."*

Questions can usually be answered by applying the pertinent rule to the facts just as it would be applied in any phase of professional accounting practice.

An effort is made in this book to explain the basic reasoning and purpose underlying each of the provisions of the Code.

*Opinion No. 14, page 208.

Reference to other chapters should enable the reader in most instances to apply the several rules to ethical questions that arise in management service work. In the long run it will undoubtedly be to the advantage of the accounting profession if, in the field of management services, as in all the other fields of its activities, it exercises care to maintain scrupulously all professional and ethical standards—competence, independence and integrity, and the professional attitude.

The fact that CPAs do have professional standards of competence and responsibility which are enforceable, not only by professional societies, but to a considerable extent under state law, will add to the confidence with which the public will engage them to render management services, as well as other types of professional accounting work.

To undertake management services as a "business" while simultaneously carrying on an accounting practice as a "profession" would undoubtedly create confusion and would dilute the prestige of the certified public accountant in both fields.

PART THREE

Relations with Others

Chapter 8

RELATIONS WITH CLIENTS

A CLIENT unavoidably puts himself in the hands of the professional practitioner whom he retains. He cannot evaluate the practitioner's technical skill or professional judgment. Therefore, the rule of *caveat emptor* cannot apply. The very nature of the relationship puts the professional practitioner in a position of trust and confidence. He should exercise no less care in dealing with the affairs of his clients than he would in dealing with his own.

The Institute's Code of Professional Ethics does not fully define the responsibilities of a certified public accountant to his client, although a few of the rules do relate directly to the interests of clients.

Sec. 76 — GENERAL OBLIGATIONS TO CLIENTS

In addition to the specific obligations imposed by the Code, the CPA owes it to his client to be competent, honest, loyal, independent and solicitous.

Competence. The obligation to be competent to do the work that is undertaken for a client is discussed at length in Chapter 2. It will be noted there that the law imposes on practitioners a duty to be as well equipped to do their work as others in the same calling may reasonably be expected to be. The ethical responsibility goes beyond the law. A CPA should not hesitate to suggest that other professional aid be enlisted if he believes in his heart that it is in the client's interest to do so.

Honesty. A CPA should not take personal advantage or profit from his knowledge of his client's affairs, without the client's consent. Nor should he accept exorbitant fees, even though the client may be innocently willing to pay them.

Loyalty. A CPA should not abandon a client, or "let him down," once the relationship has been established. He should not refuse to help a client, or withdraw from an engagement which has not been completed, merely because of personal pique, or because of fear that the engagement will not be as profitable as expected. The CPA is not, of course, obliged to complete an engagement at his own expense if it seems probable that the client will be unable or unwilling to pay a reasonable fee.

A CPA is justified in withdrawing from an engagement, however, for several reasons: (1) if he believes the client is concealing essential information from him, or is embarked upon a course of conduct which is illegal or immoral; (2) if the client persistently ignores the CPA's advice in material matters, or puts impediments in his path which prevent him from serving the client effectively; (3) if the CPA believes his own honor, self-respect or reputation may be jeopardized or he may be subjected to legal action because of his relationship with the client.

Independence. A CPA should be independent in the sense that he should not be dominated by his client. He should not accept uncritically the client's own statements of his financial affairs. He should give candid advice, even though it may be unpalatable. At the risk of losing the engagement, the CPA should insist on a course of action which he thinks is right, though the intensity of his insistence may vary with the importance of the matter under consideration.

Solicitude. Solicitude is the state of being anxious or concerned over something—in this case the client's welfare. Professional practitioners should not think of themselves as engaged simply in selling their time at a price which is competitive in the "market." It is not enough that a CPA complete a job in a workmanlike manner. He should go beyond the limits of his contract by giving thoughtful consideration to the needs of his client and attempting to help him in every practicable way.

Sec. 77 — CONFIDENTIAL RELATIONSHIP

"A member or associate shall not violate the confidential relationship between himself and his client." Thus reads Rule 1.03 of the Institute's Code of Professional Ethics.

The relationship between the CPA and his client is essentially confidential. The CPA, by the very nature of his work, is admitted to knowledge of his client's most private business and financial affairs. Like the physician, he is often the repository of information of the most personal nature. Often he is engaged by competitors in the same line of business, each of whom would be most interested to know about the affairs of the other. It would be fatal to the CPA's own professional career, and damaging to the whole profession, if the information entrusted to him were improperly revealed. It is the accountant's duty to respect the confidential relationship with his clients. The man with a loose tongue, the man who cannot keep a secret, should never attempt to practice public accounting.

Although Rule 1.03 mentions only the accountant-client relationship, the injunction applies to the disclosure of *any* confidential information to which the CPA may be given access in his professional capacity. For example, the prohibition applies both to prospective clients and to former clients. It applies to the CPA's employees as well as to himself.

The necessity of discretion will be recognized instinctively by anyone entering the practice of public accounting. It has been emphasized again and again in the professional literature. It is one of the first things that CPAs teach their young assistants. It is not uncommon to have them sign a "code of secrecy." Many CPAs will not even voluntarily disclose the names of their clients.

Sec. 78 — PRIVILEGED COMMUNICATIONS

Many of the questions requiring interpretation of Rule 1.03 arise when a client is engaged in litigation, or when the certified public accountant discovers that a client is doing something wrong.

Not infrequently CPAs are asked to testify in lawsuits, particularly in cases in which partners or minority stockholders are suing for a greater share of the profits, or for damages based on alleged malfeasance of directors. The CPA who has served as auditor of the company whose affairs are under consideration should never testify voluntarily against the management in such a matter. The information in his possession was acquired solely because he was engaged as a trusted professional practitioner and he should not violate that trust. He may, however, be required to testify under subpoena, and in this case he has no choice but to yield to the compulsion of the law.

Communications between CPA and client are not "privileged" under the common law, as are those of physicians, clergymen and lawyers. In some states, however, there is a statutory privilege. The accountancy law of Kentucky, for example, contains the following provision:

> A certified public accountant or public accountant shall not be required by any court to divulge information or evidence which has been obtained by him in his confidential capacity as such.

There is a question, however, whether a provision of a state law of this nature would be held valid in the Federal jurisdiction. The Federal courts have held that a state statute conferring privileged status on communications to accountants does not apply to a Federal administrative proceeding.* The basis of these decisions is that there is no common law privilege for communications from clients to accountants, which the Federal courts might be required to recognize, and that there is no Federal statute or rule of court making the state statute applicable to Federal administrative proceedings. Consequently, such provisions in state laws would not accord privileged status to communications to an accountant in connection with a Federal Internal Revenue Service proceeding involving the client's tax returns.

However, Federal courts would probably apply statutory provisions for privileged communications in Federal civil cases in which jurisdiction of the court is based upon diversity of citizenship of the litigants.**

Privileged communication clauses also appear in the accountancy laws of Alaska, Arizona, Colorado, Florida, Georgia, Illinois, Iowa, Louisiana, Maryland, Michigan, Nevada, New Mexico, Pennsylvania, Tennessee and Puerto Rico.

Falsone v. *United States* 205 F. 2nd 734 (5th Cir. 1953); *Dorfman* v. *Rombs,* 218 F. Supp. 905 (N.D. Ill. 1963); *Federal Trade Commission* v. *St. Regis Paper Co.,* 304 F. 2nd 731 (7th Cir. 1962).

**Palmer* v. *Fisher,* 228 F. 2nd 603 (7th Cir. 1955); *Berdon* v. *McDuff,* 15 F.R.D. 29 (E.D. Mich. 1953); *Krizak* v. *W. C. Brooks & Sons, Inc.,* 320 F. 2nd 37 (4th Cir. 1963); *Massachusetts Mutual Life Insurance Co.* v. *Brei,* 311 F. 2nd 463 (2nd Cir. 1962).

There is a difference of opinion within the profession as to whether or not statutory provisions creating privileged communications between clients and CPAs are desirable. It is universally agreed that a CPA should not voluntarily disclose any information in his possession about a client's affairs, but there is some doubt whether it is in the public interest to impede the courts in the administration of justice by preventing them by law from calling CPAs as witnesses. On the other hand, confidence that what is told an auditor in his professional capacity will be held inviolate should not only enable him to obtain all the information necessary for the conduct of an examination but should place him in a position to perform the maximum service to his client. This too is in the public interest.

It has also been argued that the granting of privileged status to communications between a CPA and his client might tend to undermine the CPA's independence as auditor. If the CPA were prevented by law from disclosing information revealed to him by his client he might be inhibited in giving an objective opinion on the financial statements.

To meet this objection a provision was incorporated in the Pennsylvania Accountancy Law in 1961 which in effect made privileged all information derived by a CPA from all professional services, except for the auditing and reporting functions.

Sec. 79 — OWNERSHIP OF WORKING PAPERS

What applies to oral disclosures by an accountant applies with equal force to his working papers and other documents in his possession containing information about a client's affairs. These papers should be guarded with the utmost diligence and scrupulously kept from the eyes of outsiders. It has been held that working papers are the property of the accountant himself,* and not even the client can require their surrender. Many accountancy laws also contain provisions to this effect.** In the absence of statutory privilege, however, working papers may be required by subpoena to be produced in court, even though they remain the accountant's property. For his own protection it has been suggested that in such cases the accountant make copies of the working papers for his own files.

Some certified public accountants, particularly in doing what is known as "write-up work," include many details of accounts in their working papers which do not appear in the client's books. Such details should be incorporated in the client's records. If this has not been done the CPA should make his working papers available to the client when occasion requires.

The Internal Revenue Service and other government agencies often request opportunity to review a CPA's working papers. Such requests should always be cleared with the client before they are granted. The CPA or his representative should always be present when the working papers are reviewed so that no schedules may be extracted without his knowledge and no alterations made in the working papers.

The committee on professional ethics has ruled that a member selling an accounting practice has a duty under Rule 1.03, pertaining to confidential relations, first to obtain permission of each client before making available to the purchaser working papers, tax returns and other confidential documents.†

---

* *Ipswich Mills* v. *Dillon*, 157 NE604 (Supreme Court of Massachusetts), July 5, 1927. See also the references in "The Ownership of Accountant's Working Papers," by the Institute's committee on state legislation, *The Journal of Accountancy*, January 1956, pages 74-76.

**Alaska, Arizona, California, Colorado, Florida, Hawaii, Kentucky, Maryland, Massachusetts, Missouri, Nebraska, Nevada, New Hampshire, Ohio, Oregon, Pennsylvania, Rhode Island, Tennessee, Utah, Virginia, Washington, West Virginia, Wisconsin, Puerto Rico and the Virgin Islands.

† Opinion No. 3, page 192.

Sec. 80 — WHEN CPA MAY MAKE DISCLOSURES
RELATED TO HIS WORK

If a certified public accountant is sued for negligence, or if he finds it necessary to sue a client for a fee, he may properly disclose to the court, orally or by reference to his working papers, such information as to the scope of his work or the nature of his service as may be necessary to defend himself or to establish the justice of his claim. He might be held guilty of unprofessional conduct, however, if on such an occasion he made gratuitous disclosures of his client's affairs unrelated to the question under litigation.

What is the CPA's duty if he discovers serious wrongdoing on the part of a client, of a nature which cannot be corrected or be disclosed in the financial statements or the accountant's report? One choice he has is simply to withdraw from the engagement. He was engaged because he could be trusted, and he must not violate that trust, though it be reposed in him by a client who proves to be unworthy.

There are occasions, however, when the auditor may discover facts about the conduct of employees or even officers of a client company which he may feel obliged to report to higher authority—the president or the board of directors. While CPAs are not expected to be informers, they cannot properly ignore situations which have a potentially adverse affect on the company's financial position.

A CPA may also be obliged to disclose a client's announced intention to commit a crime. Even the common law privilege of communications to attorneys does not extend to information concerning the client's contemplated criminal acts.* Canon 37 of the American Bar Association's canons of professional ethics states in effect that a lawyer may properly disclose a client's announced intention to commit a crime, in order to prevent the act or protect those threatened. However,

United States v. *Bob,* 106F. 2nd 37, 40 (2nd Cir. 1939).

before a CPA makes any such disclosure regarding his client's criminal intentions, he should consult with both his own legal counsel and the Institute's committee on professional ethics.

It should be restated here that the rules of the Treasury Department do not require a CPA who is an enrolled agent to reveal a client's failure to comply with the law or regulations governing determination of income taxes, but only to notify the client of such failure (see Chapter 6, page 86).

Sec. 81 — COMMISSIONS, BROKERAGE AND
FEE-SPLITTING

A specific application of the general ethical obligation not to take personal advantage or profit from knowledge of a client's affairs is provided by Rule 3.04 of the Code of Professional Ethics, which reads as follows:

> Commissions, brokerage, or other participation in the fees or profits of professional work shall not be allowed or paid directly or indirectly by a member or associate to any individual or firm not regularly engaged or employed in the practice of public accounting as a principal occupation.

> Commissions, brokerage, or other participation in the fees, charges or profits of work recommended or turned over to any individual or firm not regularly engaged or employed in the practice of public accounting as a principal occupation, as incident to services for clients, shall not be accepted directly or indirectly by a member or associate.

Protection of the interests of clients is a major purpose underlying this rule. It is also designed to fortify the accountant's independence and the professional attitude. But a major motive behind it is to avoid situations which might lead clients to suspect either that CPAs were paying commissions, which ultimately come out of the client's pocket, to laymen who helped them obtain engagements, or that their CPAs were enriching themselves indirectly, at the client's expense, by accepting commissions from vendors of goods or services, the purchase of which the CPA recommended to the client.

Even if a client did not object to the payment of a commission, there is an important reason why the CPA should not accept it. The basis of his relationship with the client is confidence. The client trusts him, or he would not have him around the place. If the client accepts his recommendation for the purchase of tabulating equipment, or some other product or service about which the CPA might be expected to know more than the client himself, he has a right to assume that the CPA has the client's interests in view. If he finds that the CPA has accepted a commission from the vendor, the client may wonder whether this particular product was really the best one for his purpose or whether the CPA's recommendation was actuated in part by the hope of personal gain.

The same reasoning would prohibit a CPA from accepting a "finder's fee" from the other party when he is acting on behalf of a client in the purchase, sale, or merger of a business.

Recommending accounting machinery or computers or other products or services may be a legitimate part of the professional service rendered by the CPA. Compensation for the time and effort which he devotes to choosing the most suitable facilities should be included in the fee which the client pays him. In these circumstances, the client will not question the objectivity with which the recommendation was made.*

Sec. 82 — CONTINGENT FEES

Rule 1.04 of the Code of Professional Ethics reads as follows:

> Professional service shall not be rendered or offered for a fee which shall be contingent upon the findings or results of

*For additional discussion of this rule see Opinion No. 6, page 194.

such service. This rule does not apply to cases involving Federal, state, or other taxes, in which the findings are those of the tax authorities and not those of the accountant. Fees to be fixed by courts or other public authorities, which are therefore of an indeterminate amount at the time when an engagement is undertaken, are not regarded as contingent fees within the meaning of this rule.

One purpose of this rule is to protect the CPA against the possibility of being influenced, or appearing to be influenced, by what might amount to a financial interest in the outcome of a business transaction to which his professional work is related. Another purpose is to protect clients against exorbitant fees.

If a CPA accepted an engagement to audit and express an opinion on financial statements of a company which intended to issue securities for sale to the public, with the understanding that his fee would be a percentage of the proceeds from the sale of the securities (which would necessarily be contingent on approval of the registration statements by the Securities and Exchange Commission and successful consummation of the underwriting), the objectivity of the CPA in expressing an opinion on the financial statements might be questioned with good reason.

The same reasoning applies not only in matters involving the expression of opinions on financial statements on which third parties might rely, but in accounting engagements in which only the client may be interested. For example, imagine a situation in which a CPA was engaged to make a cost analysis and suggest ways of reducing costs, the amount of the fee to be a percentage of the savings the client might realize by adoption of the CPA's recommendations. The CPA in such a situation would be exposed, or would appear to be exposed, to the temptation to make recommendations which might be against the long-range interests of the client, merely in order to increase the amount of the immediate savings and therefore the amount of the fee.

There is no difference of opinion in the accounting profession on the impropriety of contingent fees for accounting and auditing work in general. However, Rule 1.04 contains an exception with regard to "cases involving Federal, state, or other taxes, in which the findings are those of the tax authorities and not those of the accountant." The probable reason for this exception is that, in representing taxpayers before the Treasury Department, CPAs practice side by side with lawyers and with other enrolled agents. The rules of the Treasury Department and the canons of ethics of the American Bar Association both permit contingent fees, subject to certain conditions. It may have seemed unreasonable to impose on CPAs, through the Institute's Code of Ethics, any more rigid restrictions on fee arrangements than the Treasury itself or the Bar Association imposed on other practitioners before the Department.

However, the language of the Institute rule appears to attempt to justify the exception regarding tax cases on the ground that "the findings are those of the tax authorities and not those of the accountant." It can be reasoned that in assisting the taxpayer to establish a claim for a refund or contest an additional assessment, the CPA is not in the position of an independent auditor expressing an opinion on which third parties may rely, but is rather an expert in tax accounting, helping the taxpayer to establish precisely what his taxable income is. The government does not rely on the accountant's findings, but makes whatever investigations it considers necessary before reaching its own conclusions. Therefore, it may be argued, there is no question here of exposure to temptation or of jeopardizing public confidence in the accountant's independence. The CPA will, of course, tell the truth or forfeit his right to practice before the taxing authorities. But the question whether his judgment may be swayed by his own financial interest in winning the case is not significant here, it might be contended, because it is not the CPA's judgment, but the findings of the government agents or the courts which will finally determine the amount of income to be taxed.

It is difficult to resolve what appears to be an inherent contradiction within the rule. It says, on the one hand, that a CPA should be protected against the possibility or appearance of being influenced by a financial interest in the outcome of an auditing or accounting engagement, in which the interests of investors, creditors, or his client might conflict with his own. On the other hand, it says that there is no necessity for protecting him against the possibility of such an influence in a tax engagement, when the interests of the client, the Federal Government and, to an extent, the general public might conflict with his own.

The traditional justification for contingent fees is that they permit citizens to obtain professional assistance who otherwise could not afford it. The Treasury Department's rule says:

> An enrolled attorney or agent shall not enter into a wholly contingent fee agreement with a client for representation in any matter before the Internal Revenue Service unless the client is financially unable to pay a reasonable fee on any other terms.*

Reflecting the attitude of the legal profession, Drinker says that "... contingent fees are sanctioned in proper cases in order to enable clients to secure a competent lawyer, where otherwise they would not, in all probability, be able to do so."**

Contingent fees, however, are usually expressed in terms of a percentage of the amount which may be "saved" or "won" for the client. There is always the possibility under such an

---

* Treasury Department Circular #230, Section 10.37(b).
**Drinker, *Legal Ethics*, page 176n.

arrangement that the fee will be exorbitant. Why should it not be possible for a client who cannot afford to retain a professional practitioner unless he wins his case, to make an agreement to pay a reasonable or even a generous fee if he is successful, with the understanding that he will pay no fee if unsuccessful—but without tying the fee to the amount of the settlement?

Section 10.37(a) of Treasury Department Circular #230 forbids an enrolled attorney or agent to charge a manifestly unreasonable fee for representation of a client in any matter before the Internal Revenue Service. The American Bar Association's Canon 13 also attempts to guard against exorbitant fees: "A contract for a contingent fee, where sanctioned by law, should be reasonable under all the circumstances of the case, including the risk and uncertainty of the compensation, but should always be subject to the supervision of a court, as to its reasonableness."

Every fee is contingent, in a sense, upon the client's willingness and ability to pay it, and its amount may vary according to the extent of the work which it is found necessary to do. The prohibition against contingent fees is by no means intended to require that all fees be stipulated in advance of performance. Nor is it suggested that a CPA may not properly work for nothing, if he chooses to accommodate a friend who cannot afford to pay any fee.

Rule 1.04 says, "Fees to be fixed by courts or other public authorities, which are therefore of an indeterminate amount at the time when an engagement is undertaken, are not regarded as contingent fees within the meaning of this rule." In bankruptcy cases, for example, the courts must approve all fees for professional services rendered. In undertaking to render such service, the CPA may intend to charge for his work at his regular rates, but his compensation will be contingent on a court's approval. Yet this would not be a contingent fee within the meaning of Rule 1.04.

Nor is the rule intended to mean that a CPA's fees must always be based on inflexible per diem rates. In deciding what to charge for his work he may properly consider such factors as the following: the time and labor required, the novelty and difficulty of the questions involved, and the skill requisite to perform the engagement properly; the customary charges by certified public accountants for similar services; the amounts involved in the transactions to which the accountant's work relates, and the extent of benefit to the client resulting from the accountant's services; the character of the employment, whether casual or for an established and constant client.

Since it is entirely proper that a fee may be determined after the work is completed and the benefits to the client may be a factor in fixing its amount, just where is the line of demarcation between contingent fees that are prohibited and fees that are above criticism? The test to apply is whether, by prearrangement, the CPA has what amounts to a financial interest in a venture of his client, in that the CPA may receive an *exceptional* financial reward, contingent upon the success of the venture. This kind of prearrangement is improper because it may influence the accountant's judgment (or "findings"), or subject him to the suspicion that his independence has been impaired.

The Institute's committee on professional ethics at present has under consideration a proposal to eliminate from the contingent fee rule the exception regarding cases involving Federal, state, or other taxes.

Sec. 83 — ESTIMATES

A prospective client who in good faith wants some idea of the probable cost of the service he desires, is entitled to some kind of estimate of the general dimensions of the probable fee. Such an estimate may be given in the form of a probable minimum and maximum, and it may be made subject to the possible discovery of factors unknown at the time of the engagement which might require more work on the part of the CPA than he foresees when making the estimate.

Sec. 84 — FORWARDING FEES

"Forwarding fees" (payment by one CPA to another who has referred work to the first one) are discussed at greater length in Chapter 9 (see page 155). It is not regarded as unethical to give or receive such fees.

However, some CPAs refuse to accept forwarding fees on the ground that they add to the cost of an engagement to the client without adding anything of value to the work that is done. In other words, if the firm to which the work is "forwarded" must pay a fee to the firm which referred it, then the firm which does the work must charge enough to cover the forwarding fee in addition to out-of-pocket costs and partnership income.

Many CPAs believe that the practice of giving or receiving forwarding fees should be deprecated, on the ground that it might tempt a CPA to engage as correspondent a firm offering the largest fee, rather than one most competent to serve the client.

Some CPAs feel that if the audit of a branch or subsidiary of one of their firm's clients is undertaken, for the sake of convenience, by another CPA or firm nearer the scene of the examination, the latter firm is doing a favor to the former firm and should not be required to pay any forwarding fee.

Sec. 85 — SUITS FOR FEES

Suits by CPAs to collect fees from clients are not uncommon, but many CPAs as a matter of policy never sue for fees. The

Institute's Code of Professional Ethics is silent on this subject.

It is of interest, however, that Canon 14 of the Canons of Professional Ethics of the American Bar Association says: "Controversies with clients concerning compensation are to be avoided by the lawyer so far as shall be compatible with his self-respect and with his right to receive reasonable recompense for his services; and lawsuits with clients should be resorted to only to prevent injustice, imposition or fraud."

Drinker says a lawyer "should sue for fees only when the circumstances imperatively demand it. He will find it wise ... in the long run, not to accept any fee from an honest client greater than the client thinks he should pay."*

Among leaders of the accounting profession the same view is gaining strength.

Sec. 86 — SENDING INFORMATION TO CLIENTS

One means of evidencing an interest in clients' affairs, which is used not infrequently by CPAs, is to send them information which the practitioner believes would be of interest. The prohibitions against advertising and solicitation do not impede the sending of legitimate information to clients; for example, reprints of articles from professional journals, or speeches, or pamphlets prepared by the American Institute or other professional societies which might be helpful or interesting to the client concerned (see Section 1 of Opinion No. 9, page 197).

It is considered preferable to send such material with a personal note. Stamping of the name of the CPA on the material itself is regarded as improper (see Opinion No. 1, page 191). If any doubt is possible, the source of the material should be made known.

It has been held by the committee to be a violation of Rule

*Drinker, *Legal Ethics*, page 171.

3.01 to send to the client desk calendars, desk blotters, or other articles which are not informative but are clearly intended for display in the client's office, and which bear the name of the CPA who sent them.

Sec. 87 — BASIC CONCEPTS OF CLIENT RELATIONS

In summary, the CPA has certain specific obligations to his clients which are imposed on him by the Code of Professional Ethics. He must maintain his confidential relationship with clients. He must not accept commissions from, or share fees with, nonpractitioners. The amount of his fees should not be contingent on the findings or results of his service.

Beyond the specifics of the Code, however, the CPA has general obligations to his clients. If he thinks he is not competent to undertake an engagement, he should suggest that other assistance be obtained. He should not take personal advantage of his knowledge of his clients' affairs. He should not abandon a client or "let him down." His attitude toward clients should be characterized by fairness and candor, and he should help them in every practicable way.

Chapter 9

RELATIONS WITH FELLOW PRACTITIONERS

A LL professions stress the importance of cordial relations among their members. There are good reasons for this. The advancement of the profession as a whole—and therefore the improvement of its service to the public—depends to a large extent on a fraternal sense of goodwill and mutual confidence among the individuals who practice it. Goodwill and mutual confidence are strengthened by adherence to ethical standards and by the observation of professional etiquette and courtesy.

Sec. 88 — PROFESSIONAL RIVALRY

Excessive rivalry among practitioners would weaken or destroy the very characteristics which distinguish a profession from a business—the standards of competence and independence, the professional attitude, and solicitude for clients would all be under strain.

The standard of competence requires a readiness to refer work to specialists or call them in for consultation when appropriate. Rather than risk the loss of a client to a colleague called in for special service, a general practitioner might prefer to struggle along and do his best even with unfamiliar subject matter.

The standard of independence requires that the CPA shall not subordinate his judgment to that of his client. The accountant who knows that another CPA is knocking at his client's door might be less inclined to stand up against the wishes of his client.

The professional attitude requires renunciation of the promotional methods of the commercial world: advertising, solicitation and payment of commissions. Otherwise pressures would develop to evade the rules, or at least to ignore their spirit, while conforming only with the letter.

Solicitude for a client's welfare would soon wither away if every engagement had to be obtained solely on a price basis.

All this would be bad for the public, as well as for the profession. There is no need for codes of ethics in areas where the rule of "let the buyer beware" can be applied. However, in a field of personal service where technical skill, sound judgment and pride in achievement are the major ingredients of the product, the recipient of the service is necessarily unable to evaluate it for himself. He must put himself in the hands of the professional practitioner.

This is not to say that the practitioner has a lifelong monopoly of every client who engages him. Competition exists in the professions, since the client is free to change advisors whenever he thinks that the service is inadequate or the fees excessive. The Code of Professional Ethics places no impediment in the way of the public in its search for service of the kind it wants, at a price it can afford to pay. All the Code does is restrain the members of the profession from aggressive economic warfare, which in the end would destroy the qualities which make the profession what it is.

Sec. 89 — NEED FOR COOPERATION IN IMPROVEMENT OF THE ART

Good relations within a profession are essential for other reasons. A free interchange of information and opinion is essential to the continued enrichment of the profession's body of knowledge. Successful professional men do not make a secret of what they have learned from the hard lessons of experience. They do not patent their ideas and discoveries. In speeches at professional meetings, in articles in professional journals, in cooperative publishing efforts,* individual members of the profession contribute what they know for the improvement of the group. Some accounting firms have even contributed their own training materials to professional societies which have used the information in the preparation of professional development courses. Only by such cooperation can the profession keep pace with the requirements of a rapidly changing economy.

A CPA has no source of information about the theory and techniques of his profession except his own limited experience and what is provided by other men who have engaged in the same kind of work.

*The willingness of CPAs to share their experience with their colleagues is evidenced by such Institute publications as *The Accounting Practice Management Handbook,* the bulletins on the *Management of an Accounting Practice,* and the series of studies on *Management Services by CPAs.* In these ventures hundreds of CPAs collaborated without compensation.

Sec. 90 — NEED FOR COOPERATION IN THE
COMMON DEFENSE

Members of the profession must work together in the "common defense." Every profession has had to resist efforts to lower the standards for admission to its ranks. The CPA certificate has acquired enviable prestige and substantial economic value. Some who could not or would not meet the requirements for certification have attempted to gain some of that prestige and that value by seeking changes in the state accountancy laws. State CPA societies have resisted these efforts, for the most part successfully, and when they have failed, they have gone to work to rebuild the standards again.

The American Institute of Certified Public Accountants has had to resist proposed Federal legislation which would have been seriously injurious to CPAs.

State and national professional organizations could not carry on such efforts successfully if they were torn by internal suspicion, jealousy and strife.

It is no coincidence that the first objective of the Institute stated in its by-laws is ". . . to unite the accountancy profession in the United States as constituted by the certified public accountants of the several states, territories, possessions, and the District of Columbia. . . ."

Unity is essential to the progress of the professions, and the Institute's Code of Professional Ethics is designed in part to encourage such unity among CPAs.

Sec. 91 — PERSONAL SATISFACTION IN
RESPECT OF FELLOWS

In addition to these considerations, one of the greatest satisfactions in a professional man's life is the knowledge that he has won the respect and good opinion of his fellow practitioners. This, to be sure, is not without practical advantages.

The late Colonel Robert H. Montgomery, one of the great leaders of the accounting profession in the United States, wrote in his memoirs:

> . . . it is far easier to rise in one's trade or profession by attendance at meetings and by friendly intercourse with those in the same line as ourselves than in any other way. I took the easy way and for many years went to every meeting of accountants I could possibly attend. And often it meant giving up desirable social functions.

> Mingling with one's competitors, being able to call many of them friends, is to me an undiluted pleasure. Recently I felt rather happy when I read this by Rudyard Kipling: "Recognition by one's equals and betters in one's own country is a reward of which a man may be unashamedly proud."*

CPAs who are respected and trusted by their colleagues are likely to be called into consultation or to have work referred to them.

Sec. 92 — DEBT TO ONE'S PROFESSION

Finally, the individual has an obligation, which all civilized people acknowledge, to contribute to the group from which he has derived benefit. Francis Bacon's classic expression is frequently quoted:

> I hold every man a debtor to his profession; from the which as men of course do seek to receive countenance and profit, so ought they of duty to endeavour themselves by way of amends to be a help and ornament thereunto.

All this leads to the conclusion that a CPA's relations with

---

*Robert H. Montgomery, *Fifty Years of Accountancy*, privately printed by the Ronald Press Company, New York, N.Y., 1939, page 61.

his colleagues should be based on fair play, courtesy, mutual respect and a sense of fraternity.

Sec. 93 — ENCROACHMENT ON THE PRACTICE OF OTHERS

Rule 5.01, prohibiting encroachment, has been discussed in part in Chapter 4 (see page 55), but this rule also has a direct bearing on relations with fellow practitioners. It reads as follows:

> A member or associate shall not encroach upon the practice of another public accountant. A member or associate may furnish service to those who request it.

A major purpose of this rule is obviously to preserve harmony within the profession. There is nothing which so disturbs a professional man as to find that his client has been approached by another. This irritation does not spring entirely from mercenary motives. It comes also from hurt pride, and is the more disturbing therefor. The relations between a CPA and his client are personal and friendly, based on mutual confidence and respect. The interloper who tries to break such a relationship, and supplant the CPA who enjoys it, may be sure of the latter's unfriendly reaction.

Encroachment causes enmity, and the organized profession is fully justified in stamping it out in the interests of the group as a whole.

Sec. 94 — NOTIFICATION OF PREDECESSOR ACCOUNTANT

Rule 5.01 states in part that a member may furnish service to those who request it. This is consistent with the principle that clients shall have the right to choose, and to change, their own professional advisors. But when a CPA succeeds another on an engagement, it has long been regarded as good manners for the successor to communicate with his predecessor. Such communication may serve to avoid any suspicion that the successor had solicited the engagement. More important, communication between the two may suggest to the succeeding practitioner why the change is being made, particularly whether the predecessor has been under pressure to do anything improper, or has information which the client hopes the new appointee will not acquire.

The Institute of Chartered Accountants in England and Wales has issued a statement to the effect that a member should not accept nomination as auditor of a company without first communicating with the former or existing auditor to inquire whether there is any professional reason why he should not accept the nomination.* A rule of conduct accomplishing the same result has been adopted by the New York State Society of Certified Public Accountants. It reads as follows:

> A member shall not endeavor, directly or indirectly, to obtain clients by solicitation, and he shall not encroach upon the practice of another public accountant. A member may furnish service to those who request it; however, a member shall not agree to perform any services for a client of another public accountant without first notifying such accountant.

A similar notification requirement has been considered but not accepted by the American Institute's membership. The question will undoubtedly receive further study on the part of the committee on professional ethics.

Sec. 95 — OFFERS TO EMPLOYEES OF OTHERS

Rule 5.03 of the Code of Professional Ethics reads as follows:

Accountancy: The Journal of the Institute of Chartered Accountants in England and Wales, October 1964, page 891.

Direct or indirect offer of employment shall not be made by a member or associate to an employee of another public accountant without first informing such accountant. This rule shall not be construed so as to inhibit negotiations with anyone who of his own initiative or in response to public advertisement shall apply to a member or associate for employment.

The strength of an accounting firm lies in its personnel—partners and staff. A well-trained staff assistant is highly valued and difficult to replace. If another firm should wish to secure the services of such a man by offering a higher salary, the least the present employer is entitled to is sufficient advance notice to discuss the matter with the employee and to attempt to retain him if this is desired. It is therefore a principle of common courtesy and fair dealing which is expressed in Rule 5.03.

Some staff assistants have complained that the rule favors employers, and operates against staff men who wish to improve their positions. They say that a man cannot seek a better job without jeopardizing the job he holds, since the present employer may resent the desire of a staff man to leave, and the prospective employer will be reluctant even to negotiate with him until the present employer has been notified. This is not required by Rule 5.03, although it is quite usual, since a prospective employer naturally desires not to give offense to a fellow practitioner.

The plain truth of the matter, however, is that secrecy in human relations provokes ill will. It is better to be frank. Lasting enmities arise from incidents which allow one man to think he has been deceived by others.

A staff accountant who has confidence in his ability should not worry about making a living. He can afford to be independent, and there is no trait which he can develop to a better advantage for a career in the profession of accounting.

Therefore, a staff man who is dissatisfied with his progress should first tell his employer. The employee may be convinced that the reason he has not been advanced is through some fault of his own and he may discover how to overcome it. If not, he is a free man, and he should not lack the courage to say that he intends to look for a better job. If the employer resents this frankness it is to his discredit. His resentment will not prevent any other CPA from offering employment to the staff man. All a prospective employer will insist upon is that the present employer shall have been put on notice of the staff man's intention.

Rule 5.03 is not intended to bind staff assistants to their jobs, and does not in fact do so. It is intended to avoid ill will among members of the profession, and thus to strengthen its unity. The rule is also intended to warn the occasional less scrupulous practitioner that he may not with impunity try to lure staff assistants from their present employers who may have taught them all that now makes them valuable. If a staff assistant of his own initiative wishes to change jobs, Rule 5.03 places no barriers in his way.

Sec. 96 — REFERRALS AND FORWARDING FEES

It has been pointed out in Chapter 5 (see page 74) that Rule 2.01 of the Code of Professional Ethics permits an Institute member to utilize work done by another CPA to whom he may have referred such work.

In such cases, the one who does the work may be compensated by the CPA who referred it, in any manner which is mutually agreeable, probably at regular rates.

Sometimes, however, the referred engagement is of such magnitude and completeness in itself that the CPA performing the work may submit his bill directly to the client. In such a case, the CPA who did the work may send the one who referred it what is known as a "forwarding fee."

A forwarding fee should not be so great as to allow an abnormally small margin of profit to the firm actually doing the work. If this happens there is a danger that the firm may be tempted to "cut corners" in order to retain its profit margin.

Drinker points out that it was once customary for a lawyer to forward a case to another lawyer and to collect one third of the fee earned by the correspondent, irrespective of any service performed or responsibility assumed by the forwarding lawyer. Canon 34 of the Canons of Professional Ethics of the American Bar Association, which was adopted to condemn this practice, reads as follows:

> No division of fees for legal services is proper, except with another lawyer, based upon a division of service or responsibility.

Bar Association committees have held that no right to a division arises from the mere recommendation of another lawyer.*

As indicated in Chapter 8 (see page 144), many CPAs do not approve forwarding fees, some considering such fees an additional charge to the client for which no additional service is received. The ethical propriety of paying or receiving forwarding fees has been challenged,** and the committee on professional ethics currently has the matter under study.

Sec. 97 — UNCOMPLIMENTARY ALLUSIONS TO
FELLOW PRACTITIONERS

The rules of ethics of many professional organizations contain admonitions against uncomplimentary allusions to fellow practitioners.†

---

* Drinker, *Legal Ethics,* page 186.
**See for example, Charles Lawrence, "Professional Responsibilities in Referral Fees," *The Journal of Accountancy,* September 1958, pages 56-60.
† John W. Cook, "Additional Rules of Professional Ethics," *The Journal of Accountancy,* February 1964, page 45.

It is a common human impulse to build oneself up by tearing down the other fellow.

For reasons outlined at the beginning of this chapter, however, it is peculiarly important to a profession that good relations among its practitioners be maintained. Uncomplimentary remarks are often carried back to the person who is their object and bad feeling is the result. Repayment in kind is not unlikely.

The person who makes an uncomplimentary remark about a fellow practitioner often fails to realize that he may lose standing in the eyes of the person to whom he makes the remark. Criticizing colleagues is not generally expected of people who claim professional stature, and may hurt the critic more than the object of his criticism.

The Institute's committee on professional ethics has considered the desirability of amending the Code to require that a member refrain from speaking unfavorably of a colleague. This question will undoubtedly receive further study.

Sec. 98 — RELATIONS WITH STAFF ACCOUNTANTS

Staff accountants employed by certified public accountants are also fellow practitioners, although they may not yet be CPAs themselves. They are therefore entitled to the same fair dealing, goodwill and respect which the certified public accountant owes to other members of his profession.

Beyond this, however, it has always been assumed that a professional man has certain ethical responsibilities toward his staff assistants, mainly in training them and assisting them to become qualified as accredited members of the profession. An employer does have some responsibility, within reasonable limits, to enable a staff accountant to obtain as diverse experience as the practice permits, to arrange his work so that he can prepare for the CPA examination, to give him the benefit of the employer's knowledge and experience insofar as practicable, and above all, to treat him as though he were a member of the profession, though admittedly a junior one, instead of merely a "hired hand."

Aside from the ethics of any particular profession, under modern business standards employers of all kinds are expected not only to grant fair compensation and provide good working conditions, with reasonable working hours and vacations, but also to let employees know how they are progressing and what they may expect in the way of advancement.

A CPA should not stand in the way of a staff accountant who has an opportunity to improve his position. He should not permit a staff accountant to work for him indefinitely if the employer knows that he is not likely to advance any further, without discussing the matter with the employee. Many CPAs help their staff accountants to obtain positions with clients if the employer does not feel that the staff accountant is likely to become a partner.

Good relations with staff accountants, like good relations with other people, enrich the lives of practicing CPAs, and pay handsome dividends as well.

Chapter 10

FORMS OF ORGANIZATION
AND DESCRIPTION

S EVERAL provisions of the Code of Professional Ethics are concerned with forms of organization and descriptions of accounting firms, and the manner in which practice may be properly carried on.

Some of these have been mentioned elsewhere in this book, but it seems desirable to bring them together in one place for convenience of reference.

Sec. 99 — PRACTICE IN CORPORATE
FORM FORBIDDEN

Rule 4.06 prohibits practice in corporate form. It reads as follows:

> A member or associate shall not be an officer, director, stock-holder, representative, or agent of any corporation engaged in the practice of public accounting in any state or territory of the United States or the District of Columbia.

159

Having imposed upon its members numerous important responsibilities to clients and to the public, the profession has found it necessary to prohibit evasion of responsibility by the practice of public accounting in corporate form.

A corporation may be sued for damages, but the liability of its stockholders is limited by law. Certified public accountants who formed a corporation for the practice of their profession might be tempted (or, equally important, they might be suspected of being tempted) to take risks which they would not assume if they were personally fully responsible for their acts. Certification of financial statements by a corporation whose employees had audited the accounts would be inconsistent with the fundamental concepts of professional relationship and responsibility.

Again, a corporation is impersonal. The public may not know who the principal stockholders are. The officers might be certified public accountants and the staff might consist entirely of experienced and able auditors, but the controlling stockholder might be a layman, whose major interest was financial gain. He would stand wholly outside the jurisdiction of the professional accounting societies or other authorities which have disciplinary power over certified public accountants under law. Free from professional control, such a stockholder might nevertheless be in a position to dictate the policies of the corporate accounting firm. If such conditions were prevalent, the whole idea of accounting as a profession might as well be abandoned. In spite of all protestations, the public would recognize it as a business, and rightly so.

Sec. 100 — PROFESSIONAL ASSOCIATIONS

In recent years most states have enacted laws permitting the formation of professional corporations or associations. The purpose of such legislation is to gain a measure of tax equity for the professional man (e.g., tax-favored retirement plans). In order to be taxable as corporations these associations must have a preponderance of corporate characteristics (centralization of management, continuity of life, free transferability of interests, etc.). In order to meet the ethical restraints of the professions, associations may have unlimited liability under the law and they may require their officers and stockholders to be professionally qualified.

Despite such efforts to comply with professional standards, there are still serious objections to the practice of public accounting in the form of a professional association. For one thing, it is doubtful that the Treasury and the courts would regard the associations as corporations for tax purposes. In fact, the Internal Revenue Service has issued tentative regulations which tend to nullify the effort to obtain the tax benefits sought by the professional incorporation laws. Another objection is that the personal element in the relationship between a professional man and his clients might be threatened by the corporate form of practice. Further, the adoption of this form of practice by the professions would appear to be motivated solely by self-interest. This could damage the professional image and invite public distrust. Finally, there would remain serious ethical questions—at least insofar as public accounting is concerned: Could the confidential relationship with clients be preserved by a corporation? Could a CPA who was a stockholder of a corporation be made responsible to professional discipline for unethical acts of the corporation? If its members were not partners, could the professional corporation issue opinions on financial statements and its stockholders legally accept a common responsibility? Because of these objections, and others too numerous to recount here, the Institute's Council has gone on record as opposing legislation authorizing the incorporation of professional accounting practices.

This does not necessarily mean that the profession is

permanently committed to the partnership form of practice. In fact, changes in the traditional form may one day be dictated by changing economic and social conditions. For the present, however, and in view of the uncertainties which still exist with regard to professional associations, the Institute's position on the subject of corporate practice remains unchanged. This means that even if permitted to do so under the laws of their states, Institute members may not, in accordance with the provisions of Rule 4.06, form a professional corporation or association for the practice of public accounting.

Sec. 101 — PARTNERSHIPS AND PARTNERSHIP STYLES

Partnership is the approved form of organization in which more than one member of a profession may practice in association.

A CPA may not form a partnership with anyone who is "not regularly engaged or employed in the practice of public accounting as a principal occupation," without violating Rule 3.04, which prohibits participation in the fees or profits of professional work by nonpractitioners. Whether or not an individual is considered to be engaged in the practice of public accounting as a principal occupation depends on several factors: his maintenance of an office or desk space, his directory listing, his possession of a license if one is required, and his availability for the performance of accounting services on a fee basis.*

Up to now, Rule 3.04 has not been invoked to prohibit a member from practicing public accounting in partnership with a public accountant not certified. In the seventeen jurisdictions where regulatory accounting legislation does not exist, anyone

*Opinion No. 6, page 194.

may legally call himself a public accountant who desires to do so. In the thirty-six "regulatory" jurisdictions persons using the title "public accountant" must be licensed under law.

A member of the Institute in partnership with one who is not a member would certainly be held responsible for any breach of the Code of Professional Ethics by the partnership or by the nonmember partner. The committee on professional ethics and the Trial Board have ruled on this question on a number of occasions.

A partnership may designate itself by the names of some or all of the members of the partnership, as, for example, "Smith, Jones & Brown," or it may include in the partnership name the names of one or more of the partners, together with the designation "& Co.," for example, "Smith, Jones & Co."

It is occasionally asked whether a sole proprietor with one or more employees may practice under a designation like "John Smith & Co." While there is no specific rule which would prohibit Institute members from using such a designation, it is misleading to imply that a partnership exists when such is not the case. In fact, use of such a designation by a sole proprietor may even be illegal. The Institute's own "Form of Regulatory Public Accountancy Bill," which it recommends to state CPA societies as a guide in planning legislation, contains a provision which reads in part as follows:

> No person shall assume or use the title or designation "certified public accountant" or "public accountant" in conjunction with names indicating or implying that there is a partnership or in conjunction with the designation "and Company," or "and Co." or a similar designation if . . . there is . . . no bona fide partnership. . . .

Occasionally partnerships adopt such designations as "The John Smith Company" or "Smith & Associates." There has been no objection to such variants.

However, the Institute's committee on professional ethics

has held that a firm of practicing CPAs should have a name denoting a personal association and that it should not adopt any nonpersonal or misleading name such as "Unique Audit Company."

Sec. 102 — DESCRIPTION OF PARTNERSHIPS

The designation "certified public accountants" may be used in conjunction with a firm name if all the partners are certified public accountants of the state in which the firm practices. If some are certified in one state and some in another, then the laws of the state in which the practice is being carried on should be consulted—provisions differ among the several states.

If all the partners of the firm are Institute members, the designation "Members of the American Institute of Certified Public Accountants" may be used in conjunction with the firm name.

Rule 4.01 of the Institute's Code of Professional Ethics reads as follows:

> A firm or partnership, all the individual members of which are members of the Institute, may describe itself as "Members of the American Institute of Certified Public Accountants," but a firm or partnership, not all the individual members of which are members of the Institute, or an individual practicing under a style denoting a partnership when in fact there be no partner or partners, or a corporation, or an individual or individuals practicing under a style denoting a corporate organization shall not use the designation "Members of the American Institute of Certified Public Accountants."

If some of the partners are Institute members and others are not, the designation "Members of the American Institute of Certified Public Accountants" may not be used in conjunction with the firm name, but the names of the individual partners who are members may be listed in the corner of the letterhead with the designation "Member, American Institute of Certified Public Accountants" following each name as appropriate.

If an Institute member does not have a CPA certificate in the state in which he resides he should seek legal counsel on the question of whether or not he may indicate his Institute affiliation on his letterhead. The reason is that holding oneself out as a "Member, American Institute of Certified Public Accountants," may be regarded as holding oneself out as a "certified public accountant" of the state in question.

Occasionally a firm may wish to show on its letterhead the names of CPAs with the firm who are not partners. Both partners and staff may be listed, provided the partners are shown first in order, followed by a line to separate them from members of the staff who may be named. In this way, the public is put on notice that those below the line have a status other than that of partner.*

Rule 4.01 prohibits the use of the designation "Members of the American Institute of Certified Public Accountants" by an individual practicing under a style denoting a partnership when in fact there be no partner or partners. Under the laws of most states the same rule would apply to the use of the designation "certified public accountants."

A member practicing as an individual may, of course, use the singular forms of description "Member, American Institute of Certified Public Accountants" and "certified public accountant."

Sec. 103 — FIRM NAMES INCLUDING NAMES
OF DECEASED PARTNERS

A partnership may continue to practice under a firm name which includes the names of partners no longer members of

*See Opinion No. 11, page 201.

the firm. This is covered in Rule 4.02, which reads as follows:

> A member or associate shall not practice in the name of another unless he is in partnership with him or in his employ, nor shall he allow any person to practice in his name who is not in partnership with him or in his employ.

> This rule shall not prevent a partnership or its successors from continuing to practice under a firm name which consists of or includes the name or names of one or more former partners, nor shall it prevent the continuation of a partnership name for a reasonable period of time by the remaining partner practicing as a sole proprietor after the withdrawal or death of one or more partners.

In proposing the above rule the committee on professional ethics interpreted the phrase "a reasonable period of time" to mean that a sole proprietor practicing under a partnership name should be able to resolve the problem within one year. If he acquired another partner, he could—at least insofar as the Institute's Code is concerned—continue to use the former partnership name, whether or not it included the name of the new partner.

If a member of a two-man partnership dies, the remaining partner could continue indefinitely to hold himself out as practicing on his own account, using the legend: "Successor to (firm name)."

Sec. 104 — PURCHASE OF PRACTICE

The question sometimes arises whether there is any objection to the purchase by a CPA of a public accounting practice of another.

The purchase of public accounting practices has been, and continues to be, a generally accepted method of acquisition. There has been no intimation by any of the professional accounting societies that there is anything unethical about it.

Sec. 105 — ASSOCIATION WITHOUT PARTNERSHIP

There is nothing in the Code of Professional Ethics which would prohibit the sharing of office space by two CPAs not actually in partnership, or to prohibit them from assisting each other in the conduct of engagements. Such arrangements, however, should be specific, and a matter of record. Each CPA should be compensated by the other for whatever time he might spend in assisting the other.

Loose arrangements of this sort might lead to a violation of Rule 4.02 (see Chapter 5, page 77).

Informal association of a certified public accountant and an accountant who is not a CPA might also lead to violation of Rule 2.01, which states that a member shall not express his opinion on financial statements unless they have been examined by him, or by a member or employee of his firm.*

Sec. 106 — SIMULTANEOUS OCCUPATIONS

Rule 4.04 reads as follows:

> A member or associate shall not engage in any business or occupation conjointly with that of a public accountant, which is incompatible or inconsistent therewith.

While Rule 4.04 has rarely been invoked in recent years, it is a necessary part of the pattern of professional conduct of CPAs. The profession could not tolerate participation by any of its members in another vocation of a kind that would cast doubt on their independence, integrity, or professional attitude as CPAs.

One can easily see a relationship here to the philosophy

*See Rule 2.01, page 185. The latter part of the rule states that under certain specific circumstances a member may utilize work done by another CPA, a firm of public accountants at least one of whom is a CPA, and qualified foreign accountants.

which supports the rules prohibiting contingent fees and financial interest in client corporations and simultaneous service as auditor and director of a corporation. If it would impair independence for an auditor to have a financial interest in the outcome of an underwriting of securities of a client, for example, it would be no less incongruous to act as the underwriter or the salesman.

A secondary objective of Rule 4.04 was undoubtedly to protect the dignity of the accounting profession. Activity as a magazine salesman, for example, might not impair one's independence as a CPA, but it certainly would not enhance the public recognition of the certified public accountant as a professional man.

As pointed out by one observer, such a restriction is necessary in order to be able to say that the practice of public accounting is definable and that it meets the various tests of professional status.*

Reference has already been made in Chapter 7 (see page 114) to Rule 4.05, which reads as follows:

> A member or associate engaged in an occupation in which he renders services of a type performed by public accountants, or renders other professional services, must observe the by-laws and Code of Professional Ethics of the Institute in the conduct of that occupation.

This means that regardless of whether or not he holds himself out as engaged in the practice of accounting, a member engaged in any other occupation in which he renders services of a type performed by public accountants must abide by the Institute's Code.

Putting Rules 4.04 and 4.05 together, it will be seen that a member may engage in the practice of accounting and may

---

*Darwin J. Casler, *The Evolution of CPA Ethics,* Michigan State University, East Lansing, Michigan, page 27.

simultaneously engage in another occupation which is not incompatible or inconsistent therewith. In that other occupation, if services of a type performed by public accountants are not offered, there is no requirement that the Institute's Code be followed.

For example, if a partner in a public accounting firm were president of a manufacturing company (which was not audited by the public accounting firm), there would be no objection if the products of the manufacturing company were advertised.

Chapter 11

CONCLUSION

THE reader hardy enough to come this far will observe that the ingredients of "professional ethics" are many and varied. The aggregation of principles, rules, interpretations, admonitions and suggestions which go under the name of "professional ethics" is a growing body of thought, which will never be completed, and within which there will always be room for differences of opinion.

Its Code of ethics reveals what a profession thinks of itself and of its place in society. The Code indicates the responsibilities which the profession voluntarily assumes, the importance which members attach to their own work, and the degree of public respect to which they think they are entitled.

The rules themselves are a composite of idealism, morality, social psychology, etiquette, and public relations. Their purposes are to attract public confidence, discourage behavior inconsistent with the image of a profession, and show the members how to get along well with clients, with the community, and with each other.

In short, "professional ethics" is concerned with human conduct and human relations. As society becomes more complex, so do its ideas of proper behavior, and the professions' ethical codes reflect this growing complexity.

Let no one be discouraged then if ethical concepts are inexact, incomplete, and difficult to apply to specific situations. The standards of human behavior in general answer to these same descriptions.

The only ground for discouragement is a tendency on the part of some practitioners to ignore the practical importance of the rules of conduct—to brush them aside as "preaching" remote from the realities of professional life.

There is no more vivid reality for any human being than his relations with others. When seen in its proper light, "professional ethics" is a guide to behavior which will lead to pleasant and rewarding relations with other people. As such, the subject merits whatever thought and study that professional practitioners can give to it.

Appendices

EXCERPTS FROM THE INSTITUTE'S BY-LAWS

Article II: Members and Associates

Section 4. Upon election each member shall be entitled to a certificate setting forth that he is a member of the Institute, but no certificate shall be issued until receipt of dues for the current year. Certificates of membership shall be returned to the Council upon suspension or termination of membership for any cause except death.

Article V: Termination of Membership or Affiliation

Section 1. Resignations of members or associates may be offered in writing at any time and shall be effective on the date of acceptance. Action upon the resignation of a member or associate in good standing shall be taken by the executive committee and, in the case of a member or associate under charges, by the trial board or a sub-board appointed to hear the case.

Section 2. A member or associate who fails to pay his annual dues or any subscription, assessment, or other obligation to the Institute within five months after such debt has become due shall automatically cease to be a member or associate of the Institute, unless in the opinion of the executive committee it is not in the best interests of the profession that his membership or affiliation be terminated in this way.

Section 3. (a) A member or associate who shall resign while

in good standing may, upon request made in writing to the Institute, be reinstated by the executive committee without a reinstatement fee.

(b) The executive committee, in its discretion, may reinstate a member or an associate whose membership or affiliation has been terminated for nonpayment of dues or any other obligation owing by him to the Institute, provided that his reinstatement shall not become effective until he shall have paid to the Institute all dues and other obligations owing by him to it at the time of such termination, and shall also have paid to it a reinstatement fee in such amount, if any, as shall have been determined by a general resolution of the Council.

(c) No person shall be considered to have resigned while in good standing if at the time of his resignation he was in debt to the Institute for dues or other obligations. A member or associate submitting his resignation after the beginning of the fiscal year, but before expiration of the time limit for payment of dues or other obligations, may attain good standing by paying dues prorated according to the portion of the fiscal year which has elapsed, provided obligations other than dues shall have been paid in full.

(d) A member or associate who has resigned or whose membership or affiliation has been terminated may not file a new application for admission but may apply for reinstatement under paragraphs (a) or (b) of this section.

Section 4. A member or associate renders himself liable to expulsion or suspension by the trial board or a sub-board thereof if

(a) he refuses or neglects to give effect to any decision of the Institute or of the Council, or

(b) he infringes any of these by-laws or any provision of the Code of Professional Ethics, or

(c) he is declared by a court of competent jurisdiction to have committed any fraud, or

(d) he is held by the trial board or a sub-board thereof to have been guilty of an act discreditable to the profession, or

(e) he is declared by any competent court to be insane or otherwise incompetent, or

(f) his certificate as a certified public accountant is suspended, revoked or withdrawn by the authority of any state, territory, or territorial possession of the United States or the District of Columbia. However, should the secretary of the Institute be of the opinion that it may be in the best interest of the Institute to terminate, without trial, the membership of a member or the affiliation of an associate whose certificate has been so suspended, revoked or withdrawn, the secretary shall refer the matter to the executive committee. In such event, the executive committee may terminate, without trial, such membership or affiliation, if it determines that it is in the best interest of the Institute to do so.

Section 5. A member or associate shall be expelled if the trial board or a sub-board thereof finds, by a majority vote of the members present and entitled to vote, that he has been convicted by a court of a felony or other crime or misdemeanor involving moral turpitude; provided, in the case of such a finding by a sub-board, its finding in this respect is not reversed by the trial board. If the court conviction shall be reversed by a higher court, such member or associate may request reinstatement, and such request shall be referred to the committee on professional ethics which, after investigating all related circumstances, shall report the matter, with the committee's recommendation, to the trial board, with respect to cases heard initially by it and cases heard by it on review of a decision of a sub-board and to the sub-board which heard the case, with respect to cases heard by such sub-board in which no request for review has been granted. Whereupon the trial board or sub-board, as applicable, may by a majority vote of the members present and entitled to vote, reinstate such member or associate.

Section 6. The Council may, in its discretion, terminate the affiliation of an international associate.

Article VI: Trials and Penalties

Section 1. Any complaint preferred against a member or associate under Section 4 of Article V shall be submitted to the committee on professional ethics. If, upon consideration of a complaint, it appears to the committee that a prima facie case is established showing a violation of any by-law or any provision of the Code of Professional Ethics or conduct discreditable to a public accountant, the committee on professional ethics shall report the matter to the secretary of the Institute, who shall summon the member or associate involved thereby to appear in answer at the next meeting of the trial board or any sub-board appointed to hear the case, except that in any case involving a prima facie showing of violation of Article V, Section 4, paragraph (f), he may, in his discretion, submit the matter to the executive committee. In the event of such submittal, the executive committee shall either terminate the membership or affiliation of such member or associate pursuant to Article V, Section 4, paragraph (f) or summon him to appear in answer at the next meeting of the trial board or any sub-board appointed to hear the case.

Section 2. If the committee on professional ethics shall dismiss any complaint preferred against a member or associate, or shall fail to act thereon within ninety days after such complaint is presented to it in writing, the member or associate preferring the complaint may present the complaint in writing to the trial board.

The trial board shall make such investigation of the matter as it may deem necessary, and shall either dismiss the complaint or refer it to the Secretary of the Institute, who shall summon the member or associate involved thereby to appear in answer at the next meeting of the trial board or any sub-board appointed to hear the case.

Section 3. For the purpose of adjudicating charges against

members or associates of the Institute, as provided in the foregoing sections:

(a) The Secretary of the Institute shall mail to the member or associate concerned, at least thirty days prior to the proposed meeting of the trial board, or any sub-board appointed to hear the case, written notice of the charges to be adjudicated. Such notice, when mailed by registered mail, postage prepaid, addressed to the member or associate concerned at his last known address, according to the records of the Institute, shall be deemed properly served.

(b) After hearing the evidence presented by the committee on professional ethics or other complainant, and by the defense, the trial board or sub-board hearing the case, by a majority vote of the members present and voting, may admonish or suspend, for a period of not more than two years, the member or associate against whom complaint is made, or by a two-thirds vote of the members present and voting, may expel such member or associate. The trial board or sub-board hearing the case shall decide, by a majority vote of the members present and voting, whether the statement of the case and the decision to be published shall disclose the name of the member or associate involved. A statement of the case and the decision of the trial board or sub-board hearing the case shall be prepared by a member or members of the trial board or the sub-board, as the case may be, under a procedure to be established by such trial board or sub-board, and the statement and decision, as released by the trial board or sub-board, shall be published in the *CPA.* No such publication shall be made until such decision has become effective, as hereinafter provided.

(c) The member or associate concerned in a case decided by a sub-board may request a review by the trial board of the decision of the sub-board, provided such a request for review is filed with the secretary of the trial board at the principal office of the Institute within thirty days after the decision of the sub-board, and shall file with such request such information as may be required by the rules of the trial board. Such a review shall not be a matter of right. Each such request for a review shall be considered by an ad hoc committee to be appointed by the chairman of the trial board, or its vice chairman in the event of his unavailability, and composed of not less than five members of the trial board who did not participate in the prior proceedings in the case. The ad hoc committee shall have power to decide whether or not such a request for review by the trial board shall be allowed, and such committee's decision that such a request shall not be allowed shall be final and subject to no further review. A quorum of such an ad hoc committee shall consist of a majority of those appointed. If such a request for review is allowed, the trial board shall review the decision of the sub-board in accordance with its rules of practice and procedure. On review of such a decision the trial board may affirm, modify, or reverse all or any part of such decision or make such other disposition of the case as it deems appropriate. The trial board may by general rule indicate the character of reasons which may be considered to be of sufficient importance to warrant an ad hoc committee granting a request for review of a decision of a sub-board.

(d) Any decision of the trial board, including any decision reviewing a decision of a sub-board, shall become effective when made, unless the trial board's decision indicates otherwise, in which latter event it shall become effective at the time determined by the trial board. Any decision of a sub-board shall become effective as follows:

(i) Upon the expiration of thirty days after it is made, if no request for review is properly filed within such thirty-day period;

(ii) Upon the denial of a request for review, if such a request has been properly filed within the thirty-day period and has been denied by the ad hoc committee; and

(iii) Upon the effective date of a decision of the trial board affirming the decision of a sub-board in cases where a review has been granted by the ad hoc committee, and the trial board has affirmed the decision of such sub-board.

Section 4. At any time after the publication in the *CPA* of a statement of the case and decision, the trial board may, with respect to a case heard by it, initially or on review of a decision of a sub-board, and the sub-board may, with respect to a case heard by it in which its decision has become effective without a review by the trial board, by a two-thirds vote of the members present and voting, recall, rescind, or modify such expulsion or suspension, a statement of such action to be published in the *CPA*.

Article IX: Trial Board and Committees

Section 2. (a) The Council shall elect from its present and former members a trial board of twenty-one members in practice, seven of whom shall be elected each year to serve for a term of three years. Vacancies shall be filled by the Council for the unexpired term. No member of the committee on professional ethics shall be a member of the trial board. A quorum shall consist of a majority of the members of the trial board.

The trial board shall elect from its members a chairman and a vice chairman, the vice chairman to serve as chairman during any period of unavailability of the chairman. It shall also elect a secretary who need not be a member of the trial board. Such elections shall be for such terms of office as the trial board shall determine. The chairman, or vice chairman, when acting as chairman, may appoint from the members of the trial board a panel of not less than five members, which may, but need not, include himself, to sit as a sub-board to hear and adjudicate charges against members or associates; subject, however, to a review of its decision by the trial board, as provided in Article VI, Section 3. A quorum of the sub-board shall consist of a majority of the panel so appointed. The trial board is empowered to adopt rules governing the practice and procedure in cases heard by it or any sub-board, and in connection with any proceedings to review a decision of a sub-board. . . .

(c) The committee on professional ethics shall consist of not less than five members, not members of the executive committee, who shall be elected by Council.

Article X: Duties of Committees

Section 3. The committee on professional ethics shall perform the duties set forth in Section 1 of Article VI and may advise anyone applying to it as to whether or not a submitted action or state of facts warrants a complaint against a member or associate of the Institute, provided, however, that if the committee finds itself unable to express an opinion, such inability shall not be construed as an endorsement of the action or state of facts.

CODE OF PROFESSIONAL ETHICS
AMERICAN INSTITUTE OF
CERTIFIED PUBLIC ACCOUNTANTS

As Amended March 4, 1965

The reliance of the public and the business community on sound financial reporting and advice on business affairs imposes on the accounting profession an obligation to maintain high standards of technical competence, morality and integrity. To this end, a member or associate of the American Institute of Certified Public Accountants shall at all times maintain independence of thought and action, hold the affairs of his clients in strict confidence, strive continuously to improve his professional skills, observe generally accepted auditing standards, promote sound and informative financial reporting, uphold the dignity and honor of the accounting profession, and maintain high standards of personal conduct.

In further recognition of the public interest and his obligation to the profession, a member or associate agrees to comply with the following rules of ethical conduct, the enumeration of which should not be construed as a denial of the existence of other standards of conduct not specifically mentioned:

ARTICLE 1: *Relations with Clients and Public*

1.01 Neither a member or associate, nor a firm of which he is a partner, shall express an opinion on financial statements of any enterprise unless he and his firm are in fact independent with respect to such enterprise.

Independence is not susceptible of precise definition, but is an expression of the professional integrity of the individual. A member or associate, before expressing his opinion on financial statements, has the responsibility of assessing his relationships with an enterprise to determine whether, in the circumstances, he might expect his opinion to be considered independent, objective and unbiased by one who had knowledge of all the facts.

A member or associate will be considered not independent, for example, with respect to any enterprise if he, or one of his partners, (a) during the period of his professional engagement or at the time of expressing his opinion, had, or was committed to acquire, any direct financial interest or material indirect financial interest in the enterprise, or (b) during the period of his professional engagement, at the time of expressing his opinion or during the period covered by the financial statements, was connected with the enterprise as a promoter, underwriter, voting trustee, director, officer or key employee. In cases where a member or associate ceases to be the independent accountant for an enterprise and is subsequently called upon to re-express a previously expressed opinion on financial statements, the phrase "at the time of expressing his opinion" refers only to the time at which the member or associate first expressed his opinion on the financial statements in question. The word "director" is not intended to apply to a connection in such a capacity with a charitable, religious, civic or other similar type of nonprofit organization when the duties performed in such a capacity are such as to make it clear that the member or associate can express an independent opinion on the financial statements. The example cited in this paragraph, of circumstances under which a member or associate will be considered not independent, is not intended to be all-inclusive. [See Opinions No. 12, 15 and 16.]

1.02   A member or associate shall not commit an act discreditable to the profession.

1.03   A member or associate shall not violate the confidential relationship between himself and his client. [See Opinion No. 3.]

1.04   Professional service shall not be rendered or offered for a fee which shall be contingent upon the findings or results of such service. This rule does not apply to cases involving Federal, state, or other taxes, in which the findings are those of the tax authorities and not those of the accountant. Fees to be fixed by courts or other public authorities, which are therefore of an indeterminate amount at the time when an engagement is undertaken, are not regarded as contingent fees within the meaning of this rule.

ARTICLE 2: *Technical Standards*

2.01   A member or associate shall not express his opinion on financial statements unless they have been examined by him, or by a member or employee of his firm, on a basis consistent with the requirements of Rule 2.02.

In obtaining sufficient information to warrant expression of an opinion he may utilize, in part, to the extent appropriate in the circumstances, the reports or other evidence of auditing work performed by another certified public accountant, or firm of public accountants, at least one of whom is a certified public accountant, who is authorized to practice in a state or territory of the United States or the District of Columbia, and whose independence and professional reputation he has ascertained to his satisfaction.

A member or associate may also utilize, in part, to the extent appropriate in the circumstances, the work of public accountants in other countries, but the member or associate so doing must satisfy himself that the person or firm is qualified and independent, that such work is performed in accordance with generally accepted auditing standards, as prevailing in the United States, and that financial statements are prepared in accordance with generally accepted accounting principles, as prevailing in the United States, or are accompanied by the information necessary to bring the statements into accord with such principles.

2.02   In expressing an opinion on representations in financial statements which he has examined, a member or associate may be held guilty of an act discreditable to the profession if:

(a) he fails to disclose a material fact known to him which is not disclosed in the financial statements but disclosure of which is necessary to make the financial statements not misleading; or

(b) he fails to report any material misstatement known to him to appear in the financial statement; or

(c) he is materially negligent in the conduct of his examination or in making his report thereon; or

(d) he fails to acquire sufficient information to warrant expression of an opinion, or his exceptions are sufficiently material to negative the expression of an opinion; or

(e) he fails to direct attention to any material departure from generally accepted accounting principles or to disclose any material omission of generally accepted auditing procedure applicable in the circumstances. [See Opinion No. 8.]

2.03   A member or associate shall not permit his name to be associated with statements purporting to show financial position or results of operations in such a manner as to imply that he is acting as an independent public accountant unless he shall:

(a) express an unqualified opinion; or

(b) express a qualified opinion; or

(c) express an adverse opinion; or

(d) disclaim an opinion on the statements taken as a whole and indicate clearly his reasons therefor; or

(e) when unaudited financial statements are presented on his stationery without his comments, disclose prominently on each page of the financial statements that they were not audited. [See Opinions No. 8, 13 and 15.]

2.04   A member or associate shall not permit his name to be used in conjunction with any forecast of the results of future transactions in a manner which may lead to the belief that the member or associate vouches for the accuracy of the forecast. [See Opinion No. 10.]

ARTICLE 3: *Promotional Practices*

3.01   A member or associate shall not advertise his professional attainments or services.

Publication in a newspaper, magazine or similar medium of an announcement or what is technically known as a card is prohibited.

A listing in a directory is restricted to the name, title,

address and telephone number of the person or firm, and it shall not appear in a box, or other form of display or in a type or style which differentiates it from other listings in the same directory. Listing of the same name in more than one place in a classified directory is prohibited. [See Opinions No. 1, 2, 4, 9 and 11.]

3.02　A member or associate shall not endeavor, directly or indirectly, to obtain clients by solicitation. [See Opinions No. 1, 9 and 11.]

3.03　A member or associate shall not make a competitive bid for a professional engagement. Competitive bidding for public accounting services is not in the public interest, is a form of solicitation, and is unprofessional.

3.04　Commissions, brokerage, or other participation in the fees or profits of professional work shall not be allowed or paid directly or indirectly by a member or associate to any individual or firm not regularly engaged or employed in the practice of public accounting as a principal occupation.

Commissions, brokerage, or other participation in the fees, charges or profits of work recommended or turned over to any individual or firm not regularly engaged or employed in the practice of public accounting as a principal occupation, as incident to services for clients, shall not be accepted directly or indirectly by a member or associate. [See Opinions No. 6 and 17.]

ARTICLE 4: *Operating Practices*

4.01　A firm or partnership, all the individual members of which are members of the Institute, may describe itself as "Members of the American Institute of Certified Public Accountants," but a firm or partnership, not all the individual members of which are members of the Institute, or an individual practicing under a style denoting a partnership when in fact there be no partner or partners, or a corporation, or an individual or individuals practicing under a style denoting a corporate organization shall not use the designation "Members of the American Institute of Certified Public Accountants."

4.02   A member or associate shall not practice in the name of another unless he is in partnership with him or in his employ, nor shall he allow any person to practice in his name who is not in partnership with him or in his employ.

This rule shall not prevent a partnership or its successors from continuing to practice under a firm name which consists of or includes the name or names of one or more former partners, nor shall it prevent the continuation of a partnership name for a reasonable period of time by the remaining partner practicing as a sole proprietor after the withdrawal or death of one or more partners.

4.03   A member or associate in his practice of public accounting shall not permit an employee to perform for the member's or associate's clients any services which the member or associate himself or his firm is not permitted to perform. [See Opinion No. 17.]

4.04   A member or associate shall not engage in any business or occupation conjointly with that of a public accountant, which is incompatible or inconsistent therewith.

4.05   A member or associate engaged in an occupation in which he renders services of a type performed by public accountants, or renders other professional services, must observe the by-laws and Code of Professional Ethics of the Institute in the conduct of that occupation. [See Opinions No. 7 and 17.]

4.06   A member or associate shall not be an officer, director, stockholder, representative, or agent of any corporation engaged in the practice of public accounting in any state or territory of the United States or the District of Columbia.

ARTICLE 5: *Relations with Fellow Members*

5.01   A member or associate shall not encroach upon the practice of another public accountant. A member or associate may furnish service to those who request it. [See Opinions No. 1, 9 and 11.]

5.02   A member or associate who receives an engagement for services by referral from another member or associate shall not discuss or accept an extension of his services beyond the specific engagement without first consulting with the referring member or associate.

5.03   Direct or indirect offer of employment shall not be made by a member or associate to an employee of another public accountant without first informing such accountant. This rule shall not be construed so as to inhibit negotiations with anyone who of his own initiative or in response to public advertisement shall apply to a member or associate for employment.

Appendix C

NUMBERED OPINIONS OF THE COMMITTEE ON PROFESSIONAL ETHICS

Opinion No. 1: *Newsletters, Publications*

Impropriety of members' furnishing clients and others with tax and similar booklets prepared by others and imprinted with firm name of member.

In the opinion of the committee, imprinting the name of the accountant on newsletters, tax booklets or other similar publications which are prepared by others and distributed by a member of the Institute does not add to the usefulness of the material to the reader. Use of the imprint, in the committee's opinion, is objectionable in that it tends to suggest (and has been interpreted by many as a means of) circumventing Rule 3.01 of the Code of Professional Ethics, which says that a member shall not advertise his services.

It is the conclusion of the committee that distribution of newsletters, tax booklets or similar publications, prepared by others, when imprinted with the name of the accountant furnishing the material, is not in the interest of the public or the profession.

The committee sees no grounds for objection to furnishing material of the type indicated to clients or others provided that such material does not carry the imprint described and provided that such distribution is limited in a manner consistent with Rules 3.02 and 5.01.

Opinion No. 2: Responsibility of Member for Acts of Others on His Behalf

> *Member may not carry out through others acts which he is prohibited from directly performing under the Institute's by-laws and Code of Professional Ethics.*

A member should not cause others to carry out on his behalf either with or without compensation acts which, if carried out by a member, would place him in violation of the Institute's code or by-laws. To illustrate this principle, the committee has ruled that a member would be in violation of the Institute's Code of Professional Ethics if, with his approval:

1. A nonprofit organization in recognition of accounting services which had been rendered by a member placed without charge an advertisement of the firm in the organization's bulletin;

2. A bank announced to its depositors that a CPA would be at a desk on the main floor of the bank at certain hours and days during the tax season to assist customers in preparation of tax returns for a fee;

3. A trade association in its official publication announced that a certain certified public accountant, member of the Institute, who long had served the association as independent accountant, was especially well qualified and available to assist association members in dealing with accounting and tax problems peculiar to the industry.

Opinion No. 3: *Confidence of a Client*

> *Member selling accounting practice should not give the purchaser access to working papers, income tax*

returns, and correspondence pertaining to accounts being sold without first obtaining permission of client.

The seller of an accounting practice has a duty under Rule 1.03, pertaining to confidential relations, first to obtain permission of the client to make available to a purchaser working papers and other documents.

Opinion No. 4: *Authorship of Books and Articles*

Responsibility of author for publisher's promotion efforts.

Many members of the Institute are especially well qualified to write authoritatively on accounting, taxes, auditing, management and related subjects, and, in the interests of the public and the profession, are encouraged to write articles and books for publication. In the opinion of the committee it is of value to the reader to know the author's background (degrees he holds, professional society affiliation, and the firm with which he is associated). It is held that publication of such information is not in violation of Rule 3.01.

It is the opinion of the committee that a member of the Institute has the responsibility to ascertain that the publisher or others promoting distribution of his work keep within the bounds of professional dignity and do not make claims concerning the author or his writing that are not factual or in good taste.

Opinion No. 5: *Prohibited Self-Designations*

Use of title "Tax Consultant," "Tax Specialist" or similar description forbidden.

The "Statement of Principles Relating to Practice in the Field of Federal Income Taxation, Promulgated in 1951 by the National Conference of Lawyers and Certified Public Accountants," was approved by the Institute's Council. Section 5 of this statement reads as follows:

> "5. *Prohibited Self-Designations.* An accountant should not describe himself as a 'tax consultant' or 'tax expert' or use any similar phrase. Lawyers, similarly, are prohibited by the canons of ethics of the American Bar Association and the opinions relating thereto, from advertising a special branch of law practice."

Under Article V, Section 4, of the Institute's by-laws a member renders himself liable to expulsion or suspension by the trial board if he refuses to give effect to any decision of the Institute or the Council.

It is the opinion of the committee that a reasonable period of time has elapsed since the adoption of the Statement of Principles by Council within which the members could revise their stationery, directory and other listings so as to conform with the Statement.

Opinion No. 6: *Sharing of Fees*

> *Sharing of fees with individuals or firms not engaged or employed in the practice of public accounting prohibited.*

Rule 3.04 prohibits a member or associate from receiving or paying a commission or sharing fees or profits with any individual or firm not regularly engaged or employed in the practice of public accounting as a principal occupation.

The rule does not prevent the payment or receipt of compensation for public accounting services rendered by an employee or consultant, whether such services are on a part- or full-time basis and whether the method of payment is on an hourly or fixed basis or is measured by the fees or profits resulting from the engagement.

The rule does prevent the sharing of fees or profits or the payment or receipt of a commission in those cases where the recipient rendered no services unless he was regularly engaged in public accounting as a principal occupation.

The committee believes that the existence of more than one "principal occupation" presents no difficulty unless any of the occupations are incompatible with the practice of public accounting. Whether or not an individual is engaged in the practice of public accounting as a principal occupation is a question of fact. The maintenance of an office or desk space, a listing in a directory, the possession of a license if one is required, and the availability for the performance of accounting services on a fee basis are all factors in making this determination.

The fact that an individual is a certified public accountant does not of itself indicate that such individual is "regularly engaged or employed in the practice of public accounting as a principal occupation." Rule 3.04 is not intended to apply to or prevent payments to a retired partner, employee or proprietor of a public accounting firm or to the heirs or estate of a deceased partner, employee or proprietor. Moreover, Rule 3.04 does not at present prohibit a partnership by a member or associate of the Institute in public practice with a person who is not a certified public accountant.

Opinion No. 7: *Statistical Tabulating Services*

> *Members rendering statistical tabulating services are considered to be practicing public accounting and*

must therefore observe the by-laws and Code of Professional Ethics.

The committee on professional ethics has, in recent years, responded to several inquiries in regard to the possible violation of the Institute's Code of Professional Ethics by members who operate statistical tabulating service bureaus.

In practically all cases the tabulating services include or contemplate the accumulation of data to be used for accounting purposes, the maintenance of accounts, and bookkeeping services. This type of service is similar to so-called "write-up work" or bookkeeping service rendered by many public accountants.

Some members have formed separate partnerships which perform statistical tabulating services. Some of these organizations were apparently formed under the erroneous impression that the Institute's rules of ethical conduct would not be applicable.

The committee finds it is proper for members to conduct statistical tabulating service bureaus. The committee holds, however, that any such separate organization in which a member has an interest should not be permitted to do things which the member in public practice is prohibited from doing as a member of the Institute, such as advertising, soliciting business, or practicing in corporate form.

It is the opinion of the committee that any member of the Institute who has any interest in an organization which renders statistical tabulating services is either directly or indirectly rendering "services of a type performed by public accountants" and, therefore, must observe the by-laws and Rule 4.05, which requires compliance with the Code of Professional Ethics of the Institute.

Opinion No. 8: *Denial of Opinion Does Not Discharge Responsibility in All Cases*

When a member believes financial statements are false or misleading, denial of opinion is insufficient.

Rule 2.02 deals with a member's responsibilities in expressing an opinion on representations in financial statements. The rule does not, however, specifically refer to situations where an opinion is denied, either by disclaimer or by reference to the statements as "prepared without audit." When an accountant denies an opinion on financial statements under Rule 2.03, which incorporates the provisions of Auditing Statement 23,* he is in effect stating that he has insufficient grounds for an opinion as to whether or not the statements constitute a fair presentation. Rule 2.03 provides that where an opinion is denied, the accountant must indicate clearly his reasons therefor.

In a circumstance where a member believes the financial statements are false or misleading as a whole or in any significant respect, it is the opinion of the committee that he should require adjustments of the accounts or adequate disclosure of the facts, as the case may be, and failing this the independent accountant should refuse to permit his name to be associated with the statements in any way.

Opinion No. 9: *Responsibility for Firm Publications and Newspaper and Magazine Articles*

Members responsible for distribution of firm literature and for information supplied to the public press.

1. Newsletters and firm literature on special subjects
   This refers to house organs and publications on accounting,

*Now incorporated in Statements on Auditing Procedure No. 33.

tax accounting, articles of business interest or related subjects distributed under the auspices of, or through the facilities of, an individual or a firm for the information of clients and/or staff. The committee believes that these publications serve a useful purpose in keeping clients informed and in maintaining client relations. It does not believe that this medium should be curtailed, but the distribution of such material must be properly controlled. Distribution should be restricted to staff members, clients, lawyers of clients, bankers and others with whom professional contacts are maintained. Copies may also be supplied to nonclients who specifically request them, and to universities if the material is of educational value, and does not violate the restriction in Section 4 relating to the glorification of the individual or firm.

If requests for multiple copies are received, the firm should ascertain the intended distribution and the number of copies supplied should be limited accordingly. In granting requests for multiple copies, the individual or firm preparing the publications must assume the responsibility for any unethical distribution by the party to whom they are issued.

2. Internal publications

This includes bulletins, pamphlets, etc., containing announcements of changes in staff, activities of partners and staff members, staff training articles and other matters intended for internal consumption. Because of the nature of these publications the committee does not consider outside distribution to be a major problem. However, if distribution goes beyond internal consumption, it is subject to the restrictions stated in Section 1.

3. Staff recruitment brochures

The committee is of the opinion that the distribution of staff recruitment brochures should be limited to college placement officials, students considering interviews, and other job applicants. The material should be prepared in a dignified manner and its purpose should be to assist the college graduate in evaluating the opportunities offered by the prospective employer, and answering questions pertaining to the scope of operations, staff training, possibilities for advancement, working conditions, location of offices, etc.

4. Newspaper and magazine articles regarding firms or members of the profession

Statements made by CPAs on subjects of public interest and which contribute to public awareness of the profession should be encouraged. Members who become aware that their names or the names of their firms are to be mentioned in the public press, or in magazine articles, should apprise the author of the limitations imposed by our code of ethics. Every effort should be made to assist the author in assembling material so that the articles are factually correct and directed to improving the image of the profession and do not glorify the individual or firm or distinguish it from others in practice.

A member who is interviewed by a writer or reporter is charged with the knowledge that he cannot control the journalistic use of any information he may give. Information regarding the size of the firm, types of services which it renders, clients being served, location of offices, etc., serves no purpose other than to glorify the firm in the eyes of the reader. The same would apply to the individual if the type of information submitted goes beyond basic background material that pertains to his personal biography and his civic and other public service activities.

Deliberately cultivated publicity with respect to professional attainments will constitute a clear violation of Rule 3.01 of the Code.

Opinion No. 10: *Responsibility of Members for Pro Forma Statements and Forecasts Under Rule 2.04*

> *In preparing for management any special purpose financial statement anticipating results of future operations, a member must disclose the source of the information used and the major assumptions made, and he must indicate that he does not vouch for the accuracy of the forecast.*

Rule 2.04 provides that "A member or associate shall not permit his name to be used in conjunction with any forecast of the results of future transactions in a manner which may lead to the belief that the member or associate vouches for the accuracy of the forecast."

The ethics committee is well aware that pro forma statements of financial position and results of operation, cost analyses, budgets and other similar special purpose financial data, which set forth anticipated results of future operations, are important tools of management and furnish valuable guides for determining the future conduct of business.

The committee is of the opinion that Rule 2.04 does not prohibit a member from preparing, or from assisting a client in the preparation of, such statements and analyses. However, when a member associates his name with such statements and analyses, or permits his name to be associated therewith, there shall be the presumption that such data may be used by parties other than the client. In such cases, full disclosure must be made of the source of the information used, or the major assumptions made, in the preparation of the statements and analyses, the character of the work performed by the member, and the degree of responsibility he is taking. Such disclosure should be made on each statement, or in the member's letter or report attached to the statements. The letter or report of the member must also clearly indicate that the member does not vouch for the accuracy of the forecast. It is the opinion of the committee that full and adequate disclosure would put any reader of such statements on notice and restrict the statements to their intended use.

Opinion No. 11: *Advertising and Indication of Specialty Prohibited*

> *Advertising prohibitions relating to announcements, directories, business stationery, business cards, and office premises.*

In the opinion of the committee on professional ethics, Rule 3.01 prohibits a member or associate from advertising his professional attainments or services through any medium. The rule clearly prohibits the publication of an announcement, also referred to as a "card," or advertising in the usual form in newspapers, magazines, or other public media. It prohibits imprinting members' names, or the firm names of members, on tax booklets or other publications prepared by others. It further prohibits the association with a member's name of such phrases as "tax consultant," "tax expert," "management services," "bank auditor" and any other designations which indicate the special skills that a member possesses or particular services which he is prepared to render. It does not prohibit the use of the firm affiliation and the CPA designation in connection with authorship of technical articles and books, and it does not prohibit publicity which is of benefit to the profession as a whole.

The committee recognizes, however, that there are media, which may or may not be available to the public generally, in which it is both professional and desirable for a member's name to appear under certain circumstances. Such media include card announcements, directories, business stationery, business cards, and office premises. The committee's views on the uses of such media are as follows:

1. Announcements
   a. Announcements of change of address or opening of a new office and of changes in partners and supervisory personnel may be mailed to clients and individuals with whom professional contacts are maintained, such as lawyers of clients, and bankers.
   b. Such announcements should be dignified, and fields of specialization are not permitted to be included in the announcements.

2. Directories
   a. *General.*
      (1) A listing in a classified directory is restricted to the name, title (certified public accountant), address, and telephone number of the person or firm, and it shall not appear in a box, or other form of display, or in a type or style which differentiates it from other listings in the same directory.
      (2) Listing of the same name in more than one place in a classified directory is prohibited, and, where the classified directory has such headings as "Certified Public Accountants," or "Public Accountants," the listing shall appear only under one of those headings. Each partner's name, as well as the firm name, may be listed.
   b. *Yellow (or business) section of classified telephone directories.*

      Listings are permitted only in the classified directories which cover the area in which a bona fide office is maintained. Determination of what constitutes an "area" shall be made by the state societies in the light of local conditions.

e. Trade associations and other membership directories.

    (1) Listings of members in such directories are restricted to the information permitted in 2(a)(1) and 2(a)(2) above, and, if classified, are further restricted to a listing under the classification of "Certified Public Accountants" or "Public Accountants."

    (2) Where the directory includes geographical as well as alphabetical listings, a member may be listed in such geographical section in addition to the listing permitted above.

3. Business stationery

    a. Information appearing on a member's stationery should be in keeping with the dignity of the profession. It shall not include a listing of areas of specialization of the member or his firm, and separate stationery for tax or management services, or other specialized departments of the firm, is prohibited.

    b. *The stationery may include:*

        (1) The firm name, names of partners, names of deceased partners and their years of service, and names of staff men when preceded by a line to separate them from the partners.

        (2) The letters "CPA" following the name, the use of the words "Certified Public Accountant(s)," the address (or addresses) of office(s), telephone number(s), cities in which other offices and correspondents are located, and membership in professional societies in which all partners are members.

        (3) The public accountant designation of "Accountants and Auditors" in place of "CPA" or "Certified Public Accountant(s)" where state law or partnership affiliation does not permit such use.

    c. In the case of multi-office firms, it is suggested that the words "offices in other principal cities" (or other appropriate wording) be used instead of a full list of offices. Also, it would be preferable to list only the names of partners resident in the office for which the stationery is used.

4. Business cards
   a. Business cards may be used by partners, sole practitioners and staff members. They shall be limited to the name of the person presenting the card, his firm name, address and telephone number(s), the words "certified public accountant(s)" or "CPA" and such words as "partner" or "manager," but without any specialty designation.

   b. Members not in public practice may use the letters "CPA" after their names when acting as treasurer, controller, or in other internal accounting capacities for an organization, but shall not do so when engaged in sales promotion, selling, or similar activities.

5. Office premises
   a. Listing of the firm name in lobby directories of office buildings, and printing it on entrance doors within the building, or on the entrance to a member's office if located other than in an office building, are solely for the purpose of enabling interested parties to locate such office. The listing should conform to the size and style of other listings in the same building and should be in good taste and modest in size.

   b. The use of the words "income tax," or other specialized wording, in connection with the office of the member, including special illumination of such lettering, and signs on windows (except where such window is adjacent to the entrance), walls, building fronts, or transportation equipment used by the member(s) shall constitute advertising and shall be deemed to be a violation of the rule.

6. Help Wanted Advertisements
   a. An advertisement for "help wanted" in any publication shall not be in the form of display advertising when the name of a member or associate, or of a firm of which he is a partner, appears anywhere in the advertisement. In display advertising the use of telephone number, address, or newspaper box is permissible.

   b. In help wanted classified advertisements, other than display, the name of the firm, member, or associate should not appear in bold face type, capital letters, or in any other manner which tends to distinguish the name from the body of the advertisement.

   c. If a firm advertises for specialists, the advertisement must not convey the impression that specialized services are being offered to the public.

7. Situations Wanted Advertisement
A member or associate shall not advertise for employment in such a manner as to indicate that he is soliciting engagements as a public accountant.

   a. If the purpose of the advertisement is full-time employment as an accountant for a public accounting firm or in private industry, or per diem services to public accounting firms, statements of qualifications are permitted. Such phrases as "tax expert," "financial specialist," or any statement of self-glorification will not be permitted.

   b. An advertisement in a publication of general circulation for part-time services for which a fee is charged or per diem services (except to public accounting firms) is considered a violation of Rule 3.01.

c. An advertisement should not appear under such headings as "Business Services" or "Professional Services." It should not be of the display type and response should be directed to a box, address or telephone number.

Opinion No. 12: *Independence*

> *Auditor's responsibility to avoid relationships which to a reasonable observer might suggest a conflict of interest; propriety of member's rendering tax and management advisory services to clients on whose financial statements he expresses an independent opinion.*

Rule 1.01 of the Code of Professional Ethics states in part that "a member or associate, before expressing his opinion on financial statements, has the responsibility of assessing his relationships with an enterprise to determine whether, in the circumstances, he might expect his opinion to be considered independent, objective, and unbiased by one who had knowledge of all the facts."

Questions have arisen as to what relationships with an enterprise might be regarded by a reasonable observer, who had knowledge of all the facts, as those involving conflicts of interest which might impair the objectivity of a member in expressing an opinion on the financial statements of the enterprise. The committee does not believe that normal professional or social relationships would suggest such a conflict of interest in the mind of a reasonable observer.

In 1947 the Council of the American Institute said in an official statement on independence:

> Independence is an attitude of mind, much deeper than the surface display of visible standards.

It also said:

> In the field of auditing, the certified public accountant is under a responsibility peculiar to his profession, and that is to

maintain strict independence of attitude and judgment in planning and conducting his examinations, and in expressing his opinion on financial statements. . . . It has become of great value to those who rely on financial statements of business enterprises that they be reviewed by persons skilled in accounting whose judgment is uncolored by any interest in the enterprise, and upon whom the obligation has been imposed to disclose all material facts. . . .

While endorsing the Council's statement that independence is an attitude of mind, the committee recognizes that it is of the utmost importance to the profession that the public generally shall maintain confidence in the objectivity of certified public accountants in expressing opinions on financial statements. In maintaining this public confidence, it is imperative to avoid relationships which may have the appearance of a conflict of interest.

It is this reasoning which led the Institute to include in Rule 1.01 of the Code of Professional Ethics the statements that members should not have any financial interest in, or serve as officers or directors of, clients on whose financial statements they express opinions.

The committee does not intend to suggest, however, that the rendering of professional services other than the independent audit itself would suggest to a reasonable observer a conflict of interest. For example, in the areas of management advisory services and tax practice, so long as the CPA's services consist of advice and technical assistance, the committee can discern no likelihood of a conflict of interest arising from such services. It is a rare instance for management to surrender its responsibility to make management decisions. However, should a member make such decisions on matters affecting the company's financial position or results of operations, it would appear that his objectivity as independent auditor of the company's financial statements might well be impaired. Consequently, such situations should be avoided.

In summary, it is the opinion of the committee that there is no ethical reason why a member or associate may not properly perform professional services for clients in the areas of tax practice or management advisory services, and at the same time serve the same client as independent auditor, so long as he does not make management decisions or take positions which might impair that objectivity.

Opinion No. 13: *Tax Practice*

> *Application of Code of Professional Ethics to tax practice*

It is the opinion of the committee that the Code of Professional Ethics applies to the tax practice of members and associates except for Article 2, relating to technical standards, and any other sections of the Code which relate only to examinations of financial statements requiring opinions or disclaimers.

The committee is of the opinion that the statement, affidavit or signature of preparers required on tax returns neither constitutes an opinion on financial statements nor requires a disclaimer within the meaning of Article 2 of the Code.

In tax practice, a member or associate must observe the same standards of truthfulness and integrity as he is required to observe in any other professional work. This does not mean, however, that a member or associate may not resolve doubt in favor of his client as long as there is reasonable support for his position.

Opinion No. 14: *Management Advisory Services*

> *Application of Code of Professional Ethics to management advisory services*

Inquiries have been received as to the applicability of the Code of Professional Ethics to management advisory services. It is the opinion of the committee that all the provisions of the Code of Professional Ethics apply to management advisory services, except those rules solely applicable to the expression of an opinion on financial statements.

Opinion No. 15: *Disclaimer of auditor lacking independence*

> *Member's report should state that examination was not conducted in accordance with generally accepted auditing standards.*

Inquiries have been received as to the language of an accountant's report when he is considered to be not independent under Rule 1.01. In such circumstances he is precluded from expressing an opinion on financial statements. Instead he must disclaim an opinion and indicate clearly his reasons therefor. Moreover, he should not state that he has made an examination in accordance with generally accepted auditing standards;* nor, in the opinion of the committee on professional ethics, should he describe the auditing procedures he has followed.

With the concurrence of the committee on auditing procedure, the ethics committee suggests the following disclaimer:

> Inasmuch as we have a direct financial interest in XYZ Company [or for other reason] and therefore are not considered independent, our examination of the accompanying financial statements was not conducted in accordance with generally accepted auditing standards. Accordingly, we are not in a position to and do not express an opinion on these financial statements.

*See Statements on Auditing Procedure No. 33, Chapter 3.

Opinion No. 16: *Retired Partners and Firm Independence*

> *A firm's independence is considered impaired if a retired partner, still active in the affairs of the firm, is a director or stockholder of an audit client.*

The committee on professional ethics has considered the question of an accounting firm's independence when a retired partner of the firm acquires any direct financial interest or a material indirect financial interest in an enterprise on whose financial statements the firm is expressing an opinion or when he becomes connected with such enterprise as a promoter, underwriter, voting trustee, director, officer, or key employee.

Under Rule 1.01 it is the auditor's responsibility to assess all of his relationships with an enterprise to determine whether, in the circumstances, he might expect his opinion to be considered independent, objective, and unbiased by one who had knowledge of all the facts. The committee believes that certain relationships of a retired partner with the firm of which he was formerly a partner and with a client of that firm might suggest to a reasonable observer that the firm was lacking in independence.

For example, if a retired partner remains active in the affairs of the firm, even though not officially, the independence of the firm would be impaired if he was an officer, director, stockholder, or key employee of a client on whose financial statements the firm expresses an opinion.

However, the committee believes that if a retired partner is no longer active in the firm (regardless of the fact that he receives retirement benefits), the independence of the firm would not be impaired by his being an officer, director, stockholder, or key employee of a client on whose financial statements the firm expresses an opinion, provided that the fees received from such client do not have a material effect on his retirement benefits. A retired partner who has such a relationship with a client should not be held out as being associated with his former partnership.

Opinion No. 17: *Specialization*

> *A member may form a separate partnership with non-CPA specialists in management services, provided such partnership observes the profession's Code.*

Inquiries have been received as to ethical problems arising when CPA firms enter the fields of data processing, operations research, and other management services. This broadening of services is consistent with the objective adopted by the Institute's Council in April 1961, ". . . to encourage all CPAs to perform the entire range of management services consistent with their professional competence, ethical standards and responsibility."

In expanding services into more specialized fields, CPA firms frequently find it necessary to employ or associate with technical experts who may not be certified public accountants. This creates the problem of providing these specialists with adequate recognition and responsibility within the framework of the profession's ethical standards.

Two methods of solving this problem have evolved: (1) elevating non-CPA specialists to the rank of "principals," and allowing them to participate in the profits of the firm; (2) establishing a separate partnership which does not hold itself out as practicing public accounting and therefore may have non-CPA partners.

The committee has studied each of these methods to determine whether there is any infringement of the Code of Professional Ethics, and to establish the ethical standards under which these methods may be employed.

An investigation of the designation "principals" for non-CPA specialists and of the relationship of these individuals to the firm revealed the following: (1) "Principals" are high ranking employees who receive a base salary and who share in the profits of the firm. (2) "Principals" do not make capital contributions to the firm, do not share in the losses of the firm and have no vote in, or responsibility for, partnership decisions.

The indicated characteristics do not appear to create a partnership relationship. In fact, the attorney general of at least one state has held that such noncertified individuals, designated by a firm as "principals," are not members of the partnership and that their association with the firm as "principals" was not a violation of the accountancy statute of that state.

Since these "principals" are neither CPAs nor partners, the question arises whether the relationship is in violation of Rule 3.04 (fee sharing) or Rule 4.03 (employee's performing services which the member himself is not permitted to perform).

Rule 3.04 prohibits fee sharing with "any individual or firm not regularly engaged or employed in the practice of public accounting as a principal occupation." These "principals" are, in the committee's opinion, employed in the practice of public accounting. Consequently, Rule 3.04 does not apply. As for Rule 4.03, the services performed by these specialists (e.g., data processing, operations research, etc.) are not services regulated by law. Therefore, in the opinion of the committee, it cannot be said that employees are performing services which the member himself is not permitted to perform under the law.

The committee considered whether or not, in the absence of statutory restrictions, it would be a violation of the Institute's Code of Professional Ethics to make these non-CPA specialists partners of the firm.

The ethics committee, in Opinion No. 6, has held that Rule 3.04 does not at present prohibit a member from practicing public accounting in partnership with a person who is not a certified public accountant. Therefore, in the opinion of the committee, nothing in the Institute's present Code would prohibit members from admitting these non-CPA specialists into the partnership, although in many cases state laws would preclude the partnership from practicing under professional accounting titles and from expressing opinions on financial statements.

The second method of obtaining the necessary specialists for CPA firms to expand into the management services field is the formation of a separate partnership which does not hold itself out as practicing public accounting and which is therefore not regulated under the state's accountancy statute.

As pointed out previously, the ethics committee has ruled that the Code does not presently prohibit a member from practicing public accounting in partnership with a person who is not a certified public accountant. Therefore, the committee finds in the present Code no prohibition against the formation of a separate partnership with non-CPA specialists.

However, Rule 4.05 of the Code of Professional Ethics provides that a member engaged in an occupation in which he renders services of a type performed by public accountants must observe the By-Laws and Code of Professional Ethics in the conduct of that occupation. In addition, the ethics committee has ruled that data processing, operations research and other management services are "services of a type performed by public accountants."

Therefore, the committee is of the opinion that nothing in the Institute's Code of Professional Ethics presently prohibits a member from forming, or becoming a member of, a separate partnership with non-CPA specialists for the rendering of various management services as long as such partnership observes the By-Laws and Code of Professional Ethics. Such a separate partnership would not be permitted to advertise, solicit clients, accept commissions, or do anything else prohibited by the Code. Nor would it be permitted to hold itself out on letterheads, cards, signs, etc., in directory listings or through its partnership name as specializing in a particular service.

It should be emphasized that the committee's opinion is based upon the Code of Professional Ethics as it is now constituted. The provisions of the Code relating to this area are now under study for the purpose of determining the necessity of any revisions. If the provisions in question are revised, it may be necessary to modify or withdraw this opinion.

The conclusions reached by the committee are in accord with Opinion No. 7.

SUMMARIES OF INFORMAL OPINIONS
OF THE COMMITTEE ON
PROFESSIONAL ETHICS

In addition to issuing numbered opinions, the ethics committee gives its views on matters of less general application. Members frequently submit a set of circumstances and ask the committee's guidance on the various refinements of professional ethics and etiquette. Many of the committee's rulings on such points are summarized here as an aid to CPAs who may be confronted with similar problems. It should be emphasized, however, that in the summarization process an element of distortion may have been introduced in either the member's question or the committee's reply. For this reason CPAs are urged not to place too much reliance on these rulings but to communicate directly with the committee whenever they are unable to find authoritative information on specific ethical points.

Advertising

Canned newsletter

Q. A member asks for an interpretation of Opinion No. 1. May he send canned newsletters to his clients without his imprint but with his business card clipped to the material?

A. This mode of distribution is not regarded as a violation. However, it is preferred that the material be distributed with a covering letter expressly disclaiming authorship.

Speaker's qualifications
CPA title

Q. May a member's name, professional designation and firm affiliation be given in an advertisement to promote attendance at courses or meetings at which the member is an instructor or speaker?

A. The principles given in Opinion No. 4, though they relate to the authorship of articles and books, also apply to members who are instructors or speakers. That is, background information about the author may be given, but he is responsible for seeing to it that the promotional material keeps within the bounds of professional dignity.

Candidate for office
CPA title

Q. A member intends to file for election to a local school board. May he use his CPA title in campaign literature?

A. A member may properly substantiate his claim of worthiness for public office by using his professional designation on stationery, campaign cards and window posters, to be employed in connection with his campaign.

CPA title, multiple certificates

Q. Frequently CPAs are referred to as holding certificates from many states. Is there any objection to this practice?

A. Such a practice might mislead others into believing that the number of states in which a CPA is certified has some significance with regard to his professional standing. For this reason the Institute itself refrains from any such references when preparing biographies of authors, speakers, and other members.

CPA title on automobile license plates

Q. A firm owns five cars for the use of its senior staff. These cars bear license plates with the letters "CPA." Is this a violation of the Code of Professional Ethics?

A. The use of such license plates is a form of advertising.

CPA title imprinted on checks

Q. Is there any impropriety in a member's having his name and the words "Certified Public Accountant" imprinted on his business checks?

A. There is no objection to the use of such designation on the checks of a practicing accountant, since they go only to persons with whom the accountant has some business relationship.

CPA title imprinted on checks

Q. A member has had his name and professional designation imprinted on personal checks. Since the account is maintained jointly with his wife, her name is also imprinted on the checks. Is this ethical?

A. It is not appropriate for members to use their professional designation on personal checks or other documents which bear no relation to their professional practice.

Members are encouraged to use the CPA designation — but primarily on occasions where their professional qualifications have some relationship to the material with which their names are associated.

CPA title on agency letterhead

Q. A member has been appointed national campaign chairman for an international, nonsectarian, nonprofit agency. He asks if his name, together with his CPA title, may be shown on the agency's letterhead.

A. There is nothing wrong in the member's using his professional designation in the manner indicated. In fact, the use of the professional title under such circumstances is considered to be good for the profession as a whole.

CPA title on employment agency letterhead

Q. A nonpracticing member established an employment agency for accountants. His stationery carries his CPA title. Is this a violation of the Code of Professional Ethics?

A. There is no violation here, since the member is not holding himself out as a *practicing* public accountant.

CPA title in bank's ad

Q. May the name and professional designation of a practicing
member who is an officer and a director of a bank appear
in a list of the directors in a newspaper ad when the bank
publishes its statement of condition in accordance with
state law?

A. No. A member serving on the board of directors of a bank
may show the letters "CPA" after his name on the bank's
stationery. However, it would not be desirable for such
designation to appear on material advertising the bank in
newspapers or on billboards, etc. Inclusion of the CPA's
name and professional designation might result in more advertising for him than for the bank.

Directory listing, bank auditors
Specialization

Q. A publisher wishes to compile a directory list of CPAs who
do bank accounting or auditing work, or who give tax advice or prepare tax returns for banks. Would it be proper
for an Institute member to be listed in such a directory?

A. Such a listing would constitute the advertising of professional services or attainments. The listing would violate the
principle that a member may not carry out through others
that which he is prohibited from doing directly. (See Opinion No. 2.) It would also represent an indication of specialty, which is prohibited by Opinion No. 11.

Directory listing, fraternity

Q. A member asks if he may be listed under the caption "Accountant," in a directory published by a national fraternity

of which he is a member. There is an extra charge for such a listing.

A. While Opinion No. 11 does permit listings in membership directories, a paid listing in a fraternity directory is not allowed. Opinion No. 11 contemplates complete listings of all members of the association in question. Listings obtained by the payment of a special fee are therefore a violation of Rule 3.01.

Directory listings, multiple

Q. A member requests clarification of Section 2a(2) of Opinion No. 11 (see page 202). Specifically he poses the following questions:

1. The partnership of Smith and Jones consists of Mr. Smith, a CPA, and Mr. Jones, a public accountant. If the partnership name is listed in the yellow pages of the telephone directory under "Accountants — Public," may Mr. Smith also have his name listed under "Accountants — Certified Public"?

2. If a CPA partnership is listed in the yellow pages of the telephone directory under "Accountants — Certified Public," may a partner, whose name appears in the partnership name, also list his own name separately under "Accountants — Certified Public?"

3. May a CPA partner list his name separately under "Accountants — Certified Public," if his name is not part of the partnership name which is listed under "Accountants — Certified Public"?

A. Rule 3.01 and Opinion No. 11 were not intended to prevent such listings. The answer to all three questions therefore is yes.

Directory listing, trade association
Specialization

Q. An association directory lists a number of members and member firms. Are these listings in violation of Rule 3.01, since membership in the association does not automatically place the member's name in the directory?

A. Such a listing constitutes advertising, since the firms, which are included only on request, are grouped under specialized classes of service with differentiating descriptions.

Directory listing, trade association

Q. An Institute member became an associate member of a trade association and as a consequence his firm name was listed under the heading "Accountants" on the back of a membership letter distributed by the association. The front page of this letter carries the legend: "We urge you to patronize our associate members listed on the back of this letter."

Is this a violation?

A. Such a listing is not in keeping with the dignity of the profession or with the spirit of Rule 3.01 and Opinion No. 11.

In general, there is no objection to members being listed in association directories as long as all members are listed, there is no extra charge for the listing, and the listings are not promotional in nature so that they could be viewed by others as advertising.

Directory listing, "Tax Attorney"
Specialization

Q. May a member who is also a lawyer list himself in the

certified public accountant section of the yellow pages as a "Tax Attorney"? May he have a similar listing under the attorney section of the classified telephone directory?

A. Rule 3.01 prohibits the listing of the same name in more than one place in a classified directory. This prohibition against multiple listings applies primarily to listings indicating the kind of accounting services offered. It does not prevent a member who is also a lawyer from listing under both the CPA section and the lawyer section of the classified.

In the present instance, however, the designation "Tax Attorney" is a violation of Opinion No. 11, in that it is an association with a member's name of a designation indicating the special skills he possesses or the particular services which he is prepared to render. The title in question is also a violation of Opinion No. 5 and the "Statement of Principles Relating to Practice in the Field of Federal Income Taxation, Promulgated in 1951 by the National Conference of Lawyers and Certified Public Accountants."

Directory listing, partners' names

Q. A member asks whether the listing of a firm name in the yellow pages of the telephone directory followed immediately by the name of each partner and staff member is consistent with Rule 3.01 and Opinion No. 11.

A. It is a violation of Rule 3.01 to list under a firm's name in a classified directory all CPAs associated with the firm. Such a listing represents a "form of display . . . which differentiates it from other listings in the same directory." Also, readers might be misled to believe that all CPAs in the listing are partners of the firm. However, the committee saw no objection to the listing of each CPA alphabetically in classified directories without reference to firm affiliation.

Directory listings, membership designation

Q. May a member use in directory listings the designation "Member, American Institute of Certified Public Accountants"?

A. No. Use of such a designation would tend to differentiate members from others listed, in violation of Rule 3.01 and Opinion No. 11.

Directory listing, white pages

Q. May a CPA's firm affiliation be shown after his name in the white pages of the telephone directory?

A. It would be better to omit reference to a firm name in the white pages of the phone directory. A common type of listing is to show the member's name, followed by the title "CPA," the address and telephone number of his office, and immediately thereunder the word "residence," with the address and telephone number of his residence.

Firm name in congratulatory message

Q. A member firm has been requested to buy space in the form of a congratulatory message in the program of a club's charitable work. May the firm's name be included in the message without title, address or telephone number?

A. Even though no title was included, the appearance of the firm name might have the effect of advertising. Consequently, use of the legend "Compliments of a friend" was recommended.

Firm name on theater program

Q. The name of an accounting firm was listed among the credits in a theater program. The credit read as follows: "Accounting for (name of play) by Doe and Roe, CPAs." Is this a violation?

A. If the listing was made with the knowledge and consent of the accounting firm it would be considered a violation of Opinion No. 2, which prohibits a member from carrying out through others acts which he may not perform directly.

Firm name on automobile

Q. Would it be a violation to have the name of an accounting firm painted on the sides of a station wagon used by the firm in transporting its staff to and from clients' offices?

A. This would be considered a violation of the rule against advertising.

Firm name on tax booklet

Q. A CPA firm has been retained by stock brokerage clients to prepare annually a booklet on tax phases of security transactions. The clients bear the printing costs and the accounting firm's time charges. A legend on the cover of the booklet states that it was prepared by "Jones & Smith, Certified Public Accountants." The clients mail the booklet with an end-of-the-month statement going to their customers.

Is there any objection to this practice?

A. A CPA firm may properly prepare such technical booklets for clients. The booklets may even include reference to the services rendered by the CPA firm provided the reference is dignified and in good taste so that it could not be construed as advertising. If the services were performed without charge or at reduced rates, reference to the CPA firm would be questionable.

In some cases the content and distribution of such information may go beyond the bounds of professional dignity. The test of propriety must therefore be applied in each case to determine whether or not the material is in keeping with the spirit of the Code of Professional Ethics. In the present instance, there is no violation.

"Help wanted" ad

Q. Section 6(a) of Opinion No. 11 states in effect that a "help wanted" ad shall not be in the form of display advertising when a member's name appears anywhere in the ad. Does this restriction apply to "help wanted" advertisements placed on behalf of the member's client?

A. Section 6(a) of Opinion No. 11 applies to *all* help wanted ads, including those placed by accounting firms on behalf of their clients. The use of the firm name in a display ad is prohibited even though the words "Certified Public Accountants" are omitted.

"Situations wanted" ad

Q. A question was asked about the propriety of the following ad appearing in the "Situations Wanted" column of a local newspaper: "Accountant, CPA 16 years public experience, desires part- or full-time work while establishing public practice. Tel. No. xxx."

A. The advertisement is a violation, because the reference to part-time work sought by a CPA building up a practice invites small concerns wishing public bookkeeping and tax services to retain the advertiser.

Staff training manual

Q. A firm of CPAs conducts a training program for new staff members. Training materials include an audit manual, containing a uniform set of working papers, and practical problems for the trainees to solve. Some universities have suggested that the firm print the manual and problems to be used in their auditing laboratory courses. May the firm be shown as the author of these texts?

A. There is no reason why the firm should not receive credit for preparing training materials intended for publication and donation to universities.

Signs on office premises

Q. What are the restrictions regarding the printing of an accountant's name and title on signs outside his office?

A. For a general statement on this subject see Section 5 of Opinion No. 11, page 204. In addition, rulings have been issued on the following points:

1. Although large outside signs are not permitted, a plaque or sign bearing the name and title of a CPA is unobjectionable. The letters should not be more than three or four inches high. The sign itself should be in good taste and modest in size, so that no one could view it as advertising.

2. When an office building has the customary building directory, the committee disapproves of any sign other than the regular directory listing.

3. A member firm may list partners' names on its office door and the names of the staff men, with a line separating the partners from the employees.

Signs on office premises

Q. A CPA firm plans to build its own office building and has obtained the site.

May the firm place a sign on this property reading "Future Home of Jones & Co., Certified Public Accountants"?

The sign would be legible to passing traffic.

A. Such a display would be a violation of the rule prohibiting advertising. The purpose of outside signs is to enable interested persons to locate the CPA's office, not to advertise to the general public his professional services or attainments.

Auditor's qualifications shown in report

Q. Since some CPA firms experience difficulty in securing acceptance of their reports outside of the geographical area in which they practice, a member asks if he may have an addendum to his firm's report listing the partners' qualifications as an aid to readers in other areas in evaluating the report.

A. Such a practice would violate the prohibition in Rule 3.01 against advertising one's professional attainments.

Paid for by others, report distributed by client

Q. May a member permit his client to distribute a report of the accounting firm's findings regarding the computation of appreciation or depreciation of market value of securities over a period in the past? The letter makes it clear that the CPA has restricted computations to an analysis of a definite past period.

A. While the study may not violate any rule of professional conduct, and a careful reading of the CPA's letter makes it clear that his study relates to past and not future events, it is not considered to be in the best interests of the profession for a member to lend his name to promotional material of this sort.

Paid for by others, name in client sales letter

Q. A CPA's client plans to sell a set of books. As part of the sales program, prospective buyers are offered coupons which may be used to have questions answered concerning topics covered in the books.

The client asks the CPA for a letter giving the estimated cost of answering these questions. The letter will be reproduced and used as a part of the sales literature. The letter gives the indirect cost of each question, estimated by the time and overhead involved in rendering the service.

Is there any impropriety in the use of the accountant's name in this sales venture?

A. The member should not permit a letter of the type described to be circulated by the client corporation as part of its sales literature.

Paid for by others, name in client ad

Q. The name of an accounting firm was mentioned in an advertisement in a publication with a national circulation. The ad was a solicitation of funds for needy children. Is mention of the firm's name in these circumstances a violation of the advertising rule?

A. Identification of the auditors by name in such advertising material is unethical.

Television appearances

Q. May a member appear on a television program?

A. Members should not appear on television to affirm statements that do not require auditing or other technical work. There would be no objection to a member's appearance on such a program as a televised stockholders' meeting of a corporation of which he had served as auditor, or on a state-society-sponsored tax information program.

Specialization, acquisitions and mergers
Finder's fees

Q. May an accounting firm maintain a department whose function is to bring together business merger or acquisition prospects?

A. There is no impropriety in an accounting firm's rendering services in connection with business acquisitions and mergers, provided all provisions of the by-laws and Code are observed.

For example, a member could not hold himself out as a specialist in acquisitions and mergers, nor could he advertise, solicit clients, or encroach upon the practice of other public accountants. In addition, he would be prohibited from receiving commissions or accepting fees which were contingent upon the findings or results of his services.

Specialization, taxes
Letterheads

Q. A member asks if he may show on his letterhead the words: "Enrolled to practice before the United States Treasury Department." The Treasury Department rules permit this.

A. Since the statement implies specialization in taxes, its use on letterheads or cards is discouraged.

Tax work obtained through bookkeeper

Q. A bookkeeping company has asked a CPA to prepare tax returns on the basis of work sheets provided to the company by its customers. He asks if he may enter into such an agreement. If so, may he do the returns at a fixed fee and is he required to sign them even though the taxpayer is not his client? There would be no direct contact between the CPA and the customers of the corporation nor any indication to them of his identity.

A. The member may not properly enter into such an agreement. The bookkeeping service would obtain customers by advertising and solicitation. The CPA would indirectly receive the benefit of these unethical activities. The member was cautioned that he could not carry out through others acts which he is prohibited from doing directly under the Institute's Code.

It was pointed out also that Treasury Department regulations require anyone who prepares a tax return for another taxpayer to sign a declaration that he has examined the return and found it to be true, correct, and complete. The CPA could not properly do this without having had some direct contact with the taxpayer regarding the information contained in the return.

Tax course circulars

Q. Two members wish to send circulars soliciting enrollments in a course in Federal income taxation which they are thinking of establishing. May they use their names and professional designation in these mailings?

A. Yes, but they should not show their firm's business address on the letterhead of the school. In fact, all activities of the school should be clearly differentiated from the members' accounting practice.

Distribution of firm bulletin

Q. An accounting firm publishes a monthly information bulletin on data processing for the benefit of its staff and clients. A publishing company has asked to be put on the firm's mailing list to receive all future issues of the bulletin, which will be indexed and will remain available indefinitely. May the firm accede to the publisher's request?

A. Complying with the request would inevitably lead to ethical violations, since the firm name would be mentioned in published reports on a continuing basis and would frequently be brought to the attention of the clients of other public accountants. This would not be consistent with Opinion No. 2, which states that a member may not carry out through others acts which he is prohibited from performing directly. Since the bulletin is prepared for the information of clients and staff, its distribution should be limited in accordance with Opinion No. 9.

Distribution of CPA-authored article

Q. A securities company has asked a CPA for permission to reprint and distribute an article he had written for an accounting publication summarizing the principal factors involved in making a securities issue. The summary would not be used in a sales or promotional effort but merely as an informative service to enable the securities company to acquaint a potential issuer of securities with the problems inherent in such a transaction. Distribution of the summary would be limited to corporate officials who are contemplating an underwriting and who have begun negotiations with the securities company.

If the CPA agrees to this distribution, would there be a violation of Rule 3.01?

A. Normally there would be no problem in duplicating and distributing an item that has already been printed. But if the article were to be made the subject of a sales or promotional effort, it is possible that the accountant himself might be the subject of some criticism, even though he did not distribute the article himself.

There would be no violation of the Code if the securities

company uses reprints of the article in the manner indicated.

Distribution of CPA-authored article
Trade associations

Q. May a member give permission to a trade association to publish in its membership magazine a paper which he presented at a meeting of the association? The magazine would include a reference to the author and his firm affiliation.

A. Yes. The publication of such papers benefits both the profession and the public and should be permitted. However, the member has the responsibility to see that any references to himself or his firm are such that they would not be viewed by others as advertising.

Distribution of CPA-authored article
Trade associations

Q. A member has been asked to deliver a paper before the annual meeting of a trade association. In his speech he refers to other studies prepared by his firm which relate to the subject under discussion. May he distribute copies of his paper at the meeting? May he distribute copies of the other studies prepared by his firm, or make them available, at the meeting? All papers contain a dignified reference to the authors and their firm affiliation.

A. The member may distribute copies of his speech to those attending the meeting. However, he may not distribute or make available at the meeting copies of other studies or material prepared by his firm. If, after the meeting, requests are received for such other material, the member may comply with them.

Distribution of firm literature
Trade associations

Q. Opinion No. 9 deals in part with the distribution of multiple copies of firm literature to clients and others. Members must assume responsibility for unethical distribution by anyone requesting multiple copies. Distribution is considered unethical if it includes anyone other than staff members, clients, lawyers, bankers and nonclients who have not specifically requested copies. It is asked whether requests from trade or professional associations for multiple copies of publications may ethically be met. Could an association's request be considered a request on behalf of each of its members, thus falling within the group to whom copies may properly be sent under Opinion No. 9?

A. Multiple copies of such publications should not be furnished to trade or professional associations because the member furnishing the material would be unable to control its distribution.

It was suggested that a firm could send to a trade association as many copies of such material as it wished, provided its firm name and address did not appear on the publication.

Postage meter machines

Q. What, if anything, may properly be said by Institute members in the advertisement space provided by postage meter machines?

A. Any type of advertising in the space would be improper. Members should limit the printing on their envelopes to a dignified corner card.

Confidential Relationship

Distribution of client figures
Trade associations

Q. A trade association requested a CPA firm to supply profit and loss percentages taken from the reports of the accountants' clients to be distributed to the association's members.

A. There would be no violation if the firm had the clients' permission to distribute the figures. The information should be marked as submitted with permission of the clients of the CPA firm.

Prospective client's confidence

Q. A member was approached by a prospective client who was an employee of an existing client corporation. The employee disclosed that key personnel of the organization were planning to form their own corporation in competition with their employer. Is the member obliged to preserve the employee's confidence or should he reveal the scheme to his client?

A. The member probably would not be in technical violation

of Rule 1.03 if he revealed the scheme to the client. However, the member is morally obliged to preserve a prospective client's confidence, even though not required to do so by the letter of the rule.

Reproducing public reports

Q. A member is preparing an audit case for the use of university students and asks whether it would be ethical to reproduce actual audit reports which became public record after being submitted in evidence in court.

A. The fact that certain reports may have been submitted in evidence does not mean that the client no longer considers the information to be confidential. Therefore, the client's permission should be obtained before the CPA duplicates the information.

Revealing client information to competitors

Q. A member asks if there is any impropriety in the following circumstances: Municipalities in a particular state enforce and collect a personal property tax on business inventories, fixtures and equipment, and machinery. Each municipality retains the same firm of CPAs that does its audit to examine the books and records of all businesses to be sure the proper amount has been declared. In the course of its engagement, the CPA firm will examine sales, purchases, gross profit percentages and inventories, as well as fixed asset accounts.

The member objected to these procedures on the ground that information gathered from the books and records of his clients could be inadvertently conveyed to competitors by employees of the CPA firm doing the audit.

A. It was not improper for a CPA firm to perform such services. It should be made clear to everyone concerned that CPA firms are prohibited from revealing any confidential information obtained in their professional capacity.

Revealing names of employer's clients

Q. A staff member wishes to submit his résumé to another firm from which he hopes to obtain employment. He asks if he may include as part of his experience the names of companies for which he performed audits for his present firm.

A. The mere engagement of an accounting firm is often a confidential matter between accountant and client. But if the company issues reports that are available to the public and the employer is well known as the regular auditor, there would be no objection to revealing the fact that the member had served on that assignment.

Disclosing management information to stockholders

Q. A group of former stockholders of a corporation wish to retain a member for assistance in an action against the corporation for violation of a separation agreement. This would involve use of accounting records compiled by the CPA when the corporation was his client. Since the stockholders were active in the management of the company, the member thinks that at the time he was performing services for the corporation he was representing this group of stockholders as well as the present management.

A. Since the reason for retaining the member appears to be the knowledge he has gained from a former client, acceptance of the engagement would lead to a violation of the confidential relationship between client and CPA.

Information to successor accountant
Tax return irregularities

Q. A member withdrew from an engagement on discovering irregularities in his client's tax return. He asked if he could reveal to the successor accountant why the relationship was terminated.

A. He should not reveal the condition of the client's records. He may state that he sent his former client a letter of withdrawal, but he may not give any details unless the successor accountant obtains the client's consent. If the client refuses such consent, the successor is at least on notice.

Tax return processing

Q. May a member make use of an outside service bureau for the processing of clients' tax returns? The service bureau, which is a fully computerized operation, is seeking tax work from among CPAs' existing clients. The CPA firm controls the input of information and the computer service performs the mathematical computations and prints the return. Is there any violation of the confidential relationship in the fact that client information leaves the CPA's office?

A. A member who utilizes outside services to process tax returns or other client information may not delegate his responsibility to assure the confidentiality of such information. He must take all necessary precautions to be sure that the use of outside services does not result in the release of confidential information. He should also consider the desirability of putting the client on notice when outside services are to be used.

Tax evasion by client

Q. A member learned that a client withheld from him information on a substantial part of his income, with the result that a faulty tax return was prepared and filed. What should the member do?

A. He is not obliged to inform anyone but the client that a violation has occurred. In order to protect himself from the charge of collusion, he should write the taxpayer that the additional income should be reported in an amended return. If the client refuses to correct the return, the member should withdraw from the engagement.

Fraudulent act of client

Q. A member brought suit against his client for his fee, after the client had filed a bankruptcy petition. May the member testify at the bankruptcy hearings that the client had overstated his assets?

A. Rule 1.03 prevents the accountant from volunteering testimony at the hearing but he could reveal the facts if he was subpoenaed.

Defalcation by client

Q. An accounting firm received answers to certain verification requests from the client's customers which indicated a possible defalcation. Eventually the company's president, who owned more than 50% of the outstanding stock, confessed to his attorney and to the accountants that the company had pledged 80% of the receivables as collateral security to a factor who had advanced funds equivalent to 75% of the stated value of the receivables. The president stated that the collateral was not bona fide.

The Board of Directors has been notified of this condition by the accountants, the factor has been notified by the president, and the factor's accounting firm has been notified by the factor. The accountants have withdrawn from the audit.

Are they obliged to maintain their confidential relationship with the client or should they inform the SEC, minority stockholders, or anyone else?

A. The firm handled the matter properly. Voluntary disclosure of confidential information by a CPA might be justified ethically only if it were necessary to prevent a crime not yet committed. There is no legal or ethical requirement to disclose past acts, so long as there is no affirmative act of concealment on the part of the CPA. In such a case, however, advice of counsel is recommended.

Violation of subordination agreement

Q. An accountant has a corporate client whose principal stockholder agreed to subordinate a loan of $11,000 to the corporation for the benefit of a bank which made a loan of $8,000 to the corporation. The accountant then learned that the stockholder violated the subordination agreement by withdrawing $6,000 from the corporation against the loan. Should the accountant disclose this information to the lending bank even though he is not presently called upon to prepare a financial statement?

A. The accountant is under no obligation to divulge the information to the bank unless there was an agreement to do so at the time of the loan. When he prepares the financial statements, however, he should set forth the information in a footnote to the balance sheet.

Contingent Fees

Expert witness

Q. May a member, as an expert witness in a damage suit, receive compensation based on the amount awarded the plaintiff?

A. Such an agreement would violate Rule 1.04, prohibiting contingent fees. Compensation for expert testimony may be at a per diem rate or at a fixed sum previously agreed upon.

Incompatible occupations, "finders"

Q. A member asks if he may act as a "finder" for a client in the acquisition of another company. That is, would the occupation of "finder" be considered incompatible or inconsistent with public accounting? If he may serve as "finder" would he be in violation of Rule 1.04 by charging a fee contingent upon the acquisition, and based on a percentage of the acquisition price?

A. The occupation of "finder" is not incompatible or inconsistent with public accounting. However, the payment of a contingent fee under such circumstances is not proper. The accounting firm should charge a fee commensurate with the service performed, though such fee could be in excess of the rates for regular auditing and accounting services.

Data Processing

Billing service
Solicitation

Q. A practicing member wishes to form a corporation to perform centralized billing services for local doctors.

He maintains that this service, which is similar to one currently offered and advertised by a local bank, does not constitute the practice of public accounting and that Rules 4.05 and 4.06 and Opinion No. 7 consequently do not apply. He wishes to circularize local doctors of his acquaintance, informing them of the availability of the service.

A. The activity in question does constitute service of a type performed by public accountants and consequently the member may enter this field only if the operation is conducted in accordance with the Institute's Code of Professional Ethics, which of course prohibits advertising, solicitation and practice in corporate form.

Consultant to service bureau

Q. A practicing CPA is to be retained by a corporation to

assist it in developing a tabulating service to be offered to the public. He will have no financial interest in the corporation and no representations will be made that he or any CPA is connected with the development of the tabulating service.

A. There is no violation in the member's plan.

Service bureau as client

Q. Would it be proper for a CPA to be retained by a data processing center to investigate the problems of other business units (frequently served by other public accountants) and to report to the service center his recommendations on the need for data processing equipment? The CPA would assist in the installation of the necessary equipment. He would bill his regular per diem charges to the service center.

A. Such an arrangement would be improper since it would result in the offering of CPA services under the name of a processing center, which itself advertises for and solicits clients.

There would be no objection if the service center recommended to its customers that the CPA be retained to determine the need for data processing equipment. The CPA could then bill the client for his services.

Stock ownership in service bureau

Q. A firm represented in the Institute's membership serves as the accountants for a statistical service bureau, which contemplates offering its stock to the public under an SEC registration. The firm wishes to acquire shares in the corporation which would represent not more than 10% of the total of the shares to be outstanding.

The service bureau operates like any commercial firm in that it advertises and solicits business. The bureau's management is completely independent of the accounting firm, and no member of the firm serves as officer, director, or employee of the bureau. The firm does not represent, nor will it represent in the future, any of the customers of the service bureau, other than those which it has recommended or may in the future recommend to the service bureau.

The firm understands that if it acquires stock in the service bureau it cannot express an opinion on the financial statements of the concern.

The firm believes that these circumstances comprise a different kind of situation from that contemplated in ethics committee Opinion No. 7.

A. Opinion No. 7 and Rules 4.05 and 4.06 are not intended to prevent a member from owning stock in a corporation *solely as a financial investment.* Several large corporations, through the rental of business machines, are engaged in rendering data processing services and might therefore be considered to be rendering services of a type performed by public accountants. But a member may properly own stock in such a corporation, provided he does so in accordance with the limitations described above. In the present case, there is no violation.

Partnership with non-CPA

Q. A noncertified, unlicensed accountant in a regulatory state proposes to form a partnership with a CPA for the rendering of tabulating services. The partnership will solicit business from practicing CPAs and public accountants — not from their clients. The noncertified accountant is also the sole owner of a local service bureau. There is to be no connection between this company and the proposed partnership. The partnership would operate within the framework of the profession's Code of Professional Ethics.

Is the proposed arrangement ethical?

A. A connection between the service bureau and the proposed partnership is established in that the noncertified accountant would be the owner of a tabulating service dealing with the general public, and at the same time would be a partner in a firm offering services to practicing public accountants. Such an arrangement would necessarily bring about a violation of the Institute's Code. The danger is that the service bureau might be used as a "feeder" to the public accounting practice, and the CPA involved might indirectly obtain the advantages of advertising, solicitation and other activities which he is prohibited from performing directly.

The plan was therefore not approved.

Fee sharing

Q. An accounting firm wishes to set up a data processing center by forming a joint venture with three of its clients — a bank, a professional engineering firm, and a trucking company. The joint venture would be an entity separate from the public accounting firm and would be known as the Blank Data Processing Company. If the joint venture operates at a profit and the profits are divided among the four adventurers, would this be considered a participation in the fees of professional work by nonpractitioners in violation of Rule 3.04?

A. Yes. Such services are "of a type performed by public accountants" and members rendering these services must observe all provisions of the by-laws and Code (Opinion No. 7). Since Rule 3.04 prohibits the sharing of fees with persons not engaged in public accounting as a principal occupation, the operation of such a separate organization would be prohibited, regardless of the fact that it did not advertise, solicit clients or practice in corporate form.

Also, such a joint venture with clients would jeopardize the firm's independence as auditors of those clients.

In addition, since the organization would be subject to the profession's ethical restrictions, which prohibit the indication of specialties, it would not be permitted to designate itself as a "data processing" center.

Fee Sharing

CPA-*professor*

Q. The first part of Rule 3.04 states in effect that a member may not share professional fees with anyone "not regularly engaged or employed in the practice of public accounting as a principal occupation." It is asked whether a member may share the profits of professional work with a CPA who is a full-time professor of accounting but who also does some public accounting work.

A. Many members conduct an accounting practice in addition to their full-time employment in education or industry. In general, such a member is considered to be engaged in the practice of public accounting as a principal occupation if he holds himself out as such, maintains an office, lists himself in a directory, renders services for clients, and is not engaged in another occupation which would be considered incompatible or inconsistent with public accounting. (See Opinion No. 6.)

In the situation presented, it is not a violation of Rule 3.04 for the member to share fees with the CPA-professor.

Service corporation dividends

Q. A member has the opportunity to share in the ownership of a service corporation to be organized to purchase supplies, engage and discharge personnel, and provide legal and accounting services for hospitals. He would share 49% of the stock equally with the attorneys doing the legal work. His fees would be charged to the corporation on a per diem basis, and the reports signed by him as a CPA. Does this proposal create any ethical problems?

A. Payment of part of the accountant's fee in the form of dividends would violate Rule 3.04, but there would be no objection to the proposal if he held no stock in the corporation.

Bonus or profit-sharing plan

Q. May a member share the profits of professional accounting work with his employees?

A. Rule 3.04 was intended to prevent the sharing of the profits of professional work with anyone "not regularly engaged or employed in the practice of public accounting as a principal occupation." It was *not* designed to prevent a firm from having some form of bonus or profit-sharing plan. Such plan could include participation in all profits of the firm or in a specified portion thereof. All employees may take part in the plan, or only certain classes or individuals. The practice is quite common among firms represented in the Institute's membership.

Purchase of practice
Estate of deceased practitioner

Q. In purchasing the practice of a deceased accountant, a member agrees to pay the estate a share of the profits of the practice over a specified period. Is this a violation?

A. Rule 3.04 forbids participation by nonpractitioners in the fees or profits of professional work, but payments to a widow or to the estate of a retired or deceased practitioner are not considered a violation. It would be improper, however, for a former partner's widow to be included as a partner of a CPA firm, unless she were personally professionally qualified.

Purchase of practice, seller under indictment

Q. A member asks if he may purchase the practice of another CPA who is under indictment for criminal fraud. The price is to be paid, over a period of several years, on the basis of a percentage of the fees received. If such a purchase were delayed until after the CPA's trial, would there be a violation of ethics, assuming the CPA is convicted and loses his certificate?

A. There would be no violation of the Institute's rules in the purchase of this practice, provided the CPA under indictment has the right to practice, which is presumably until his certificate is revoked. Payments for the practice which might extend to a date when the seller has lost his CPA certificate would not be considered fee-splitting with a nonpractitioner.

Commission from nonpractitioner

Q. A member proposes to render a management service to his clientele by arranging for the purchase of supplies from a supplier who offers a discount. The supplier, who is also a client, feels that the CPA's fee should be increased as compensation for providing this service. Would this constitute a violation of Rule 3.04? Would the answer be any different if the supplier was not a regular client of the CPA firm?

A. Accepting a commission from the supplier, whether or not he is a regular client, would violate Rule 3.04, which states in part that a member may not participate in the profits of work recommended to a nonpractitioner as incident to services for clients. Assisting clients to obtain the best equipment at the best price is a legitimate professional service, however, and the CPA may properly charge for the time and effort devoted to this activity.

Incompatible Occupations

Bank director

Q. May a CPA serve as director of a bank to which he is submitting opinion reports for consideration in making loans to his clients?

A. Service as a bank director has never been considered an occupation incompatible with public accounting. The CPA, of course, could not act as independent auditor of the bank, nor could he use his position as a "feeder" to his public accounting practice.

However, it should be recognized that a member serving in this dual capacity would occasionally be put in an embarrassing position. For example, he may find himself discussing the affairs of one of his clients, when he had confidential information not available to his co-directors. The CPA-bank director should abstain from voting on any matters in which any conflict-of-interest appeared to exist.

Finance company

Q. Advice is sought regarding the propriety of a CPA's conducting a public practice and also being involved in the operation of a finance company.

A. Such an arrangement is a violation of the rule against incompatible occupations. There is a danger that the finance company might serve as a "feeder" to the public accounting firm and there may be relations between clients of the accounting firm and the finance company that might cast doubt upon the independence of the accounting firm.

The firm should decide whether it wishes to conduct a public accounting practice or operate a loan company. In the event the interest in the finance company is to be disposed of, a reasonable time is permitted within which to carry out the decision.

Loan broker

Q. An insurance company asked a CPA to serve as broker in

handling industrial and commercial loans. Some of the CPA's clients might be interested in obtaining these funds. Would acceptance of the offer involve a violation of the Code?

A. The committee ruled that a member cannot act as a loan broker and independent accountant at the same time, without violating Rule 4.04.

Consumer credit company

Q. A consumer credit company purchases installment sales contracts from retailers and receives payments from consumers. May a practicing CPA serve as a director or officer of such a corporation?

A. Yes — provided he does not audit the corporation.

Collection agent
Confirmation procedure

Q. May a member send collection letters to customers of his clients?

A. The mailing of collection letters is a violation of Rule 4.04, since this occupation is incompatible and inconsistent with public accounting. Also letters of this kind tend to discredit the confirmation procedure.

Coaching course for CPA candidates

Q. A practicing member wishes to conduct a CPA coaching

course and to promote the course by mailings to other practicing public accountants.

Is there any objection to such a venture?

A. Conducting a coaching course is not incompatible or inconsistent with public accounting. Many practicing members are associated with such educational efforts.

In promoting such a course the member must be circumspect about the distribution of the advertising literature. He should keep copies of mailing lists, in case there is any question about the distribution of the course prospectus.

Employment agency

Q. A practicing member proposes to engage in a business venture in the employment agency field. He plans to supply other CPAs with accountants, bookkeepers, and related personnel. He would hire a counselor to manage the agency and his accounting practice would not be affected.

Is the proposed occupation incompatible with public accounting?

A. There would be no violation of Rule 4.04, provided the CPA's activities are limited to those described. If they extended to non-CPAs, the agency might be considered as serving as a "feeder" to his public accounting practice. The member was also cautioned against the use of his professional designation in connection with the agency, including its name.

Escheator

Q. May a member serve as an escheator and at the same time

conduct an accounting practice? His duties require him to learn whether certain corporations have property which should revert to the state in the absence of persons legally qualified to inherit or claim it. May he write to such corporations using his professional stationery?

A. There is no violation of the Institute's Code under these circumstances, unless it is shown that the member's position as escheator is used as a feeder to his public accounting practice.

If the escheator were appointed for a period of time rather than for a particular case, he should have special stationery for his duties in that appointment.

Insurance actuary
Specialization

Q. An accounting firm has acquired only that portion of an insurance brokerage firm which performs actuarial and administrative services in connection with employee benefit plans. Does this constitute a violation of Rule 4.04, regarding incompatible occupations?

A. Actuarial and administrative services in connection with employee benefit plans are a proper function of CPAs and are not incompatible with the practice of public accounting. If the organization does not advertise, solicit, or do anything else contrary to the profession's ethical standards, including the indication of specialties, there would be no objection to the arrangement. (See Opinion No. 17.)

Investment advisory service

Q. Members of an accounting partnership would like to form a corporation, with themselves as sole stockholders, to publish a service furnishing statistical information on stocks and forecasting earnings and/or stock prices, to be made available on a subscription basis. Recommendations to buy or sell would be made, and advertising would be necessary. Neither the letterhead nor the advertising of the corporation would indicate the names of stockholders nor would there be any reference to the CPA firm.

Would this be permissible if (a) conducted in the same offices as the public accounting practice or (b) conducted in different offices?

A. Simultaneous operation of an accounting practice and an investment service, either in the same office or in separate offices, would be a violation of Rule 4.04.

Investment counselor

Q. A member serves as a counselor and dealer in securities, while also conducting a public accounting practice. He asks if he is in violation of Rule 4.04.

A. Conduct of a brokerage office or that of investment counselor and dealer in securities is incompatible with the practice of public accounting. Carrying on a successful investment counseling business would require communication on business matters with clients of other CPAs, and might become a means of circumventing the rules concerning advertising and solicitation. The member should choose either one activity or the other.

Investment salesman

Q. A member wishes to serve as local representative of an open-end investment trust. His compensation would be in the form of a commission on sales. Would this arrangement violate the Code of Professional Ethics?

A. Because it would necessarily involve active solicitation of possible buyers of securities and consequently discussions of accounting and tax matters, this occupation would be incompatible with public accounting.

Securities dealer

Q. A member sells mutual funds to friends and clients. He has a license to do so by virtue of his membership in the National Association of Security Dealers, Inc. He also has a few public accounting clients.

Is there any ethical violation in this situation?

A. The sale of mutual funds is an occupation incompatible with public accounting and the member is consequently in violation of Rule 4.04.

Stock broker

Q. A member in active practice wishes to have a limited partnership interest in a brokerage firm that is a member of the New York Stock Exchange. He will invest capital on which he will receive a fixed return rather than a share of the profits. He will receive no other benefits from the firm, which in turn will receive no other benefits from him. He will not discuss securities with any customer of the brokerage firm. He will not represent either the brokerage firm in its position as underwriters or any company which the firm is underwriting.

Would such an arrangement constitute a violation of Rule 4.04, prohibiting incompatible occupations?

A. There would be no violation of the Code as long as the member was not the auditor of the brokerage firm, did not use such firm as a "feeder" to his accounting practice, and his relationship with the firm remained as outlined.

Real estate broker

Q. Is the operation of a part-time real estate business (as a broker) incompatible with public accounting?

A. If the member retains his independence as auditor and does not use the real estate business to "feed" his accounting practice, serving as a real estate broker and public accountant would not be prohibited by the Code of Professional Ethics, though such simultaneous service is not encouraged.

If it is necessary because of financial pressure for the member to have a second occupation, great care must be taken to disassociate the real estate business from the professional accounting practice, even to the point of maintaining two different offices.

State secretary of revenue

Q. As the state secretary of revenue, a member administers the state taxation system. Would this position be incompatible with an active partnership in a public accounting firm?

A. As long as the accountant refrains from appearances in connection with state tax matters of his clients and confines his tax practice to filing returns, this post is not incompatible with public accounting.

Independence

Auditor as transfer agent

Q. Can a member be considered independent when he serves his client both as auditor and as stock transfer agent?

A. The independence of an auditor who also serves as transfer agent would be jeopardized, since normally the auditor would review the work of a transfer agent employed by the client. However, there would be no conflict if the member's duties as transfer agent are solely ministerial and if no accounting work is performed which might bias his judgment as auditor.

Auditor as bank director
Incompatible occupations

Q. The partners of an accounting firm have contracted to purchase a majority of the outstanding capital stock of a state-chartered bank. They will be elected to the Board of Directors of the bank and thereafter may be elected officers and become active in the management of the bank on a part-time basis while continuing to practice public accounting.

The firm will not render an opinion on the financial statements of the bank. However, some of the bank's customers may also be clients of the accounting firm.

Are there any problems regarding (1) an incompatible occupation or (2) the firm's independence with respect to clients who are also customers of the bank?

A. The position of bank officer or director is not necessarily incompatible or inconsistent with the practice of public accounting. (See page 249.) But if it were shown that the member was using another occupation as a "feeder" to his public accounting practice, the committee would demand that the dual relationship cease.

The arrangement might also involve situations and problems which could challenge the firm's independence or at least lead to questions as to conflicts of interest. Such situations seem unavoidable unless the bank neither receives deposits from nor makes loans to any of the firm's clients. Ownership and control of a bank holding deposits of, or making loans to, the firm's clients may amount to its having a financial interest in the clients in question.

In short, the members were discouraged from proceeding with the plan.

Auditor as city councilman

Q. May a CPA serve as independent auditor of a municipality when for a part of the audit period he served as a city councilman under the city-manager type of municipal government?

A. Service as councilman would jeopardize his independence as auditor.

Auditor as commissioner

Q. Two cities have agreed to construct a sewage treatment plant which will be controlled, managed and operated by a Joint Board of Commissioners, two from each city. The

Board will have complete control over construction and operations of the plant, including setting up a system of accounts, establishing a uniform schedule of rates, and providing for an annual audit by a CPA.

A member appointed to the Board asks if he could at the same time serve as auditor of this nonprofit organization.

There is a possibility he may serve as Treasurer of the Board and would be signing all checks.

A. The member could not properly serve as auditor and member of the Joint Board.

Auditor as county executive

Q. A CPA holds a full-time elective office as the chief executive of a political subdivision of his county. He continues to practice as a CPA through his accounting office staff. May he accept engagements for certified audits of other departments of the same county?

A. The CPA could not be considered independent in connection with audits of other departments of the county in which he is serving as an executive.

Staff man as county supervisor

Q. A CPA firm serves as auditors for the following elected county offices: County Treasurer, Circuit Clerk, County Clerk, Sheriff, and County Superintendent of Schools. After the completion of the audits, the firm employed as a staff man an accountant who was also serving on the County Board of Supervisors. This Board approves all purchases and supervises the county officers. For service on the Board the staff man receives $1,000 a year.

Is there any impropriety in this situation?

A. The fact that a member of the Board of Supervisors is an employee of the firm would predispose the Board to favor the selection of the firm over others. The circumstances also might influence the conclusions of the partners or employees connected with the audit. Also any censurable act of the Board of Supervisors might result in unpleasant publicity for the firm, since the Board member, as an employee of the firm, will be regarded by the public as part of the firm's "family."

In short, the situation impairs the independence of the firm.

Auditor as supervisor

Q. A member asks if he may enter into a contract with a township to supervise office personnel of the power company and the town on a monthly fee basis, approve vouchers for payment, prepare operating reports (monthly for the trustees and quarterly for the state comptroller), and also enter into a contract to make the annual audits and render an opinion on the financial and other statements.

A. Under these circumstances the CPA would not be considered independent.

Auditor as controller

Q. A corporation which employs an Institute member as controller is audited by a firm of CPAs. The controller prepares and certifies the statements of a subsidiary corporation. Can the outside firm accept these statements for the purpose of preparing a consolidated balance sheet?

A. No. As an employee of the corporation, the controller cannot maintain his independent status.

Auditor as controller

Q. A former partner of an accounting firm has been serving as controller of one of the firm's audit clients. Since he now wishes to return to public practice, arrangements have been made for him to join the accounting firm's staff. When this takes place, he will have severed all connections with the client and will have disposed of all financial interests. He will not participate in the current audit of his former employer's financial statements. It is asked whether Rule 1.01 would prevent the firm from admitting this individual into partnership.

It is pointed out that Rule 1.01 says in effect that a member will be considered not independent with respect to an enterprise if he, or one of his partners, during the period covered by the financial statements was connected with the enterprise as an officer or a key employee. It is argued that the intent of this provision is to prevent situations where partners in public accounting firms are *simultaneously* connected with audit clients. It is therefore alleged that Rule 1.01 will permit the interpretation that no independence problem is created, so long as all of the individual's relationships with the client are severed prior to his admission into the partnership.

The firm will be called on to express an opinion in an SEC registration statement on financial statements covering a period prior to this individual's employment with the firm during which he was employed by the audit client. He will not become a partner until after the firm's examination has been completed and its report submitted on this year's financial statements. He will not participate in this year's audit or in the audit of subsequent years until the firm is satisfied that all major problems relating to transactions that he instituted have been resolved.

A. Rule 1.01 was not intended to restrict the movement of personnel between public accounting firms and their clients, though such movement can raise questions of independence. For example, if the controller of an enterprise severed his relationships with that enterprise and accepted a position as partner-in-charge of the audit of that enterprise for a period during which he served as controller, a reasonable observer might not consider him independent, objective and unbiased — even though at no time was he *simultaneously* a partner of the accounting firm and a key employee of the client.

In the present circumstances it appears that since proper precautions are being taken, independence in both fact and appearance can be maintained. The principal precaution is to provide an adequate lapse of time during which the former officer or employee of a client who is now associated with the accounting firm has no part in the audit of his former employer. The other precautions to be taken by the firm seem to assure compliance with both the letter and the spirit of Rule 1.01.

Auditor as controller

Q. A member asks if the independence of his firm would be jeopardized by having a staff employee of the firm serve as a resident auditor of the client.

A. An auditor is not necessarily lacking in independence because he or his firm has written up the client's books, made adjusting entries, and prepared financial statements. However, if an employee of an accounting firm signs checks, approves vouchers, employs and discharges personnel, or performs any other functions of management, the independence of the firm would be jeopardized.

A firm would not be considered independent with respect to any enterprise if a staff member of the firm makes management decisions or exercises the controllership function of the enterprise. (See Opinion No. 12.)

Consultant as co-trustee

Q. An accounting firm is negotiating a merger with a smaller partnership. The senior partner of the latter will not become a partner of the new firm but will serve it as a consultant. His duties will be to effect the orderly transfer of the clients from his former firm to the new firm. He may also refer clients to the new firm but will not otherwise participate in its activities. His compensation would be a fixed sum paid over a ten-year period and will be unrelated to future profits.

Will the new partnership be considered independent with respect to an enterprise if the consultant serves as a co-trustee of an estate which has a material financial interest in the enterprise?

A. Since the consultant is not a partner of the new firm, does not participate in its activities and does not share in its profits, the firm would not be considered lacking in independence.

Auditor as trustee
Financial interest

Q. An accounting firm wishes to admit to partnership a CPA who is the son of the firm's founder now deceased. The CPA owns stock in a corporation audited by the accounting firm and under his father's will was named a trustee of a trust holding stock in the corporation. The CPA plans to dispose of his personal holdings. Would his admission to partnership impair the independence of the firm with respect to the corporation?

A. In order for the accounting firm to retain its independence the CPA must not only dispose of his stock in the client company but he must also resign his position as trustee.

As long as a member has authority to vote or sell stock in a client company he (or his firm) cannot be considered independent with respect to that enterprise.

Auditor as trustee

Q. May a member serve as a trustee under a revocable living trust to a client who has a substantial interest (approximately 31%) in an audit client?

If the independence rule is intended to prohibit joint service as auditor and *voting* trustee, would it not be proper to act as trustee under a revocable living trust even when under certain conditions (such as mental incompetency of the transferor) it might be necessary for a trustee to vote the stock?

A. The CPA's independence would be impaired if he acted as

co-trustee of a trust and independent auditor of a corporation, some of whose stock was owned by the trust. As long as there are certain conditions under which the CPA might be required to vote the stock, he should not serve as independent auditor.

Auditor as executor

Q. A member has been named co-executor of an estate which has a controlling interest in a corporation audited by the member. That control is to remain with the executors as trustees until the children of the deceased reach maturity. Can the member serve as independent auditor of the corporation?

A. No. The relationship in question would impair the auditor's independence.

Auditor as co-trustee

Q. A member has been named co-executor and co-trustee under the will of a client now deceased. Among the assets under his control is 20% of the common stock of a company audited by his firm. The member has no financial interest in either the company or the estate other than through audit and executor fees. He expects to be discharged as co-executor but would continue as co-trustee. Could his firm retain its independence as auditors if he issued an irrevocable proxy to his co-executor or co-trustee to vote this particular stock?

A. The issuance of an irrevocable proxy would not assure the member's independence in these circumstances. He should either withdraw as executor and trustee of the estate, or withdraw as independent auditor for the corporation — unless the trust were to dispose of its stock ownership in the corporation.

Auditor as co-trustee

Q. A member's client, the sole stockholder of a corporation, has decided to place all of his assets including the stock of his corporation into a revocable living trust. The purpose of this trust is to facilitate the passage of assets and reduce paper work upon his death. He has asked the member to serve as a co-trustee. The client will retain full powers to vote the stock and to revoke or amend the trust in any way, including the appointment of new trustees. Until the client's death, the trustees will have no actual function except to hold nominal title to the properties in the trust. If the member accepted such a co-trusteeship, would his firm be precluded from rendering an opinion on financial statements of a corporation whose stock is owned by the trust?

A. Despite the arguments that could be made in favor of the auditor's independence in such circumstances, the member could not serve as trustee and still audit the corporation, since as a trustee he would be in theoretical control of the corporation.

It was thought that circumstances could arise where he would lose his independence if he continued to act as trustee. For example, if the trustor should become incompetent, a court might give the trustees actual control of the property. Also, in the event of the trustor's death, the trustees would continue to hold the property until death taxes and other liabilities had been paid.

Even though there may be technical compliance with Rule

1.01, a third party in possession of the facts would not in such circumstances consider the auditor independent, objective and unbiased.

Auditor as trustee of client's profit-sharing plan

Q. A member who is a trustee of a profit-sharing plan makes the relationship clear in his audit report and disclaims an opinion because of his lack of independence. He is also the auditor for the corporate client who is the sole contributor to the profit-sharing plan. Will his relationship as trustee of the related profit-sharing plan affect his ability to express an unqualified opinion on the corporate financial statements?

A. Serving in the dual capacity of independent auditor of a corporation and trustee of the corporation's profit-sharing plan would appear to be a conflict of interest in the eyes of third parties. If the company wanted to borrow funds from its own profit-sharing plan, the auditor may be put in the position of having it said that his vote was influenced by those who retain him.

Another consideration is whether funds of the profit-sharing plan were invested in securities of the client. If so, there would be an obvious conflict of interest in that the trustees of the plan would have control over stock in the client.

Also, if the trustee's fee is determined by the corporation's contributions to the plan, and if such contributions are determined by the income of the corporation (a figure attested to by the auditor), there would appear to be a conflict of interest in the member's serving in both capacities.

In summary, members should not serve in the dual capacity

of independent auditor of a corporation and trustee of the corporation's profit-sharing plan.

Auditor in retirement plan

Q. The auditor of a municipality has been offered the opportunity of joining the municipality's retirement plan. Would such action impair his independence?

A. If the accountant accepted the "employee" designation for the purpose of entering the retirement plan, there would be a strong implication that he was not independent with respect to the municipality.

Auditor as participant in client's pension plan

Q. A CPA's client wanted him to be a participant in the company's pension plan for employees. It was arranged to pay part of the accountant's fee as "wages," though at no time was the CPA an employee, stockholder, officer, or director. Now, for the first time, the CPA will be called upon to express an opinion on the company's financial statements. Will his participation in the pension plan affect his independence as auditor?

A. Yes. The long-range implications of such participation would increase the danger of his being influenced by personal considerations. The mere designation of part of his fee as "wages" would put the accountant in a compromising position. Even if he had no direct financial interest in the corporation, participation in the pension plan represents a more important interest than the ownership of a few shares of stock.

Auditor as director

Q. May a member serve in the dual capacity of director of an enterprise and independent auditor of that enterprise's profit-sharing and retirement trust?

A. An auditor who serves as a director of an enterprise could not expect third parties to consider him independent, objective, unbiased with respect to that enterprise's profit-sharing and retirement trust. As a director of the enterprise, the CPA would be in a position to vote on amendments to the trust agreement which, in the eyes of third parties, might appear to jeopardize his independence as auditor.

Auditor as "associate director"

Q. May a member be listed as "Associate Director" in published statements of his client, if he has no vote at Board meetings and receives no directors' fees?

A. If the CPA is listed as "Associate Director" in the published statements of an enterprise, whether or not he is entitled to vote or is paid for such services, it would be assumed that he was a part of the management of that enterprise and he therefore should not serve as the independent CPA. Of course, this does not prevent the CPA from attending directors' meetings to give independent advice and consultation. Nor does it prevent him from charging a fee for the time spent in performing this service.

Consultant as director

Q. A corporation's quarterly report to stockholders indicated that a CPA, described as a consultant to an accounting firm, was elected a director of the company. The accounting firm in question also served as independent auditors of the corporation's accounts. Does this situation constitute a violation of Rule 1.01?

A. Investigation revealed that the consultant was not and never had been either a partner or an employee of the accounting firm. In these circumstances the committee held that there was no impairment of independence, though there should have been no indication in the company's quarterly report that the consultant was affiliated with the accounting firm in any way.

Staff man as director

Q. A staff man of an accounting firm is a member of the Board of Directors and treasurer of a Federal savings and loan association. The staff member has no proprietary interest in the accounting firm. The firm is conducting negotiations with the savings and loan association which may lead to the performance of an opinion audit. If the engagement materializes, the firm will not use the staff member in question on the audit.

Would the firm be considered independent under these circumstances?

A. While not explicitly forbidden by Rule 1.01, the relationship in question might appear to jeopardize the firm's independence. A reasonable observer, who had knowledge of all the facts, might believe that the CPA firm was auditing and expressing an opinion on the work and decisions of one of its own employees.

The firm should therefore not accept the engagement.

Auditor as officer-director

Q. Would a member's independence with respect to a local
Boy Scout Council and a legal aid society be impaired if
he served as a director and assistant treasurer of the United
Community Chest, which serves as a federated fund-raising
organization from which the Boy Scouts and the legal aid
society receive funds?

A. Since the officer-director of the Community Chest did not
exercise managerial control over the independent organizations participating in the fund-raising organization, such
service would not jeopardize the auditor's independence
with respect to participating organizations.

Deceased partner

Q. A deceased partner of an accounting firm had been a stockholder, director and voting trustee of a company which
now wishes the firm to audit its records. The partner died
during the audit period and his interest in the company
has since been liquidated. May the new partnership express an independent opinion on the company's statements
under these circumstances?

A. A third party having knowledge of all the facts would
have no cause to question the objectivity of the firm in
conducting an examination of, and expressing an opinion on,
the financial statements of the enterprise.

Auditor as director, non-profit organization

Q. May an accounting firm perform a certified audit of a

YMCA if one of the firm's partners serves as a member of the board of directors of this charitable organization?

A. After prohibiting service as director and auditor, Rule 1.01 goes on to state that the word "director" is not intended to apply to a connection in such a capacity with a charitable, religious, civic or other similar type of non-profit organization "when the duties performed in such a capacity are such as to make it clear that the member or associate can express an independent opinion on the financial statements."

The purpose of this exception is to enable the member to audit the records of a client while he is serving on the board in a purely honorary capacity. Many fund-raising organizations like to have well-known people serving on their boards and many members have lent their names to such worthy causes.

However, serving as director and auditor of a YMCA does not seem to fall into this category. While the YMCA is a non-profit organization, the partner's position as one of the directors might not be considered a purely honorary one. He would presumably be exercising some managerial control over the work of the YMCA. If so, his duties would not be such as to make it clear that he could express an independent opinion on the financial statements. For this reason, the partner should resign as director or the firm should withdraw as independent auditors.

Auditor as director, nonprofit organization

Q. May a partner of an accounting firm serve on the board of directors of a country club without jeopardizing the firm's right to render an opinion on the country club's statements? In short, does a country club come under the exception in Rule 1.01 which permits a member to serve both as auditor and director of charitable, religious, civic, and other types of nonprofit organizations?

A. If a member expressed an opinion on the financial statements of a country club of which he or one of his partners was a director, he would then be reporting on his own stewardship. The exception made for nonprofit organizations was intended primarily to cover those situations in which a member was lending his name to a worthy cause without assuming administrative or financial responsibilities. The auditor may serve as director only "when the duties performed in such a capacity are such as to make it clear that the member or associate can express an independent opinion on the financial statements." This language of Rule 1.01 makes it clear that the objective test of independence should be applied in such cases.

Auditor as member of board of trustees, nonprofit organization

Q. Would the appointment of a partner of an accounting firm to the board of trustees of a welfare federation render the firm not independent with respect to that organization? The board of trustees approves the budget of the campaign and planning functions of the federation. It approves committee appointments made by the president. It may allocate some of its functions to subcommittees, such as finance, personnel, etc. However, all final decisions on matters of program policy and operations rest with the board of directors.

A. Since the board of trustees consists of more than sixty

members, and since the position of trustee is more honorary than managerial, a partner of the firm may serve as a trustee of the federation without impairing the firm's independence, under the exception in Rule 1.01 in favor of nonprofit organizations.

If the partner was appointed to the executive committee or the finance committee of the federation, the duties involved would no doubt be such as to jeopardize the independence of the firm with respect to the federation.

Disclaimer of opinion

Q. The disclaimer of an auditor lacking in independence recommended in ethics committee Opinion No. 15 reads as follows:

> Inasmuch as we have a direct financial interest in XYZ Company [or other reason] and therefore are not considered independent, our examination of the accompanying financial statements was not conducted in accordance with generally accepted auditing standards. Accordingly, we are not in a position to and do not express an opinion on these financial statements.

It is asked whether the following clause may be appended to the final sentence of the recommended disclaimer: "which have been prepared in accordance with generally accepted accounting principles."

A. The addition of this clause would indicate that an auditor need not be independent to express an opinion on whether or not financial statements are presented in accordance with generally accepted accounting principles. Such an indication would tend to make the disclaimer similar to the ordinary disclaimer based on scope, which similarity should be avoided. When the auditor is lacking in independence, he should treat the statements somewhat as if they were unaudited; and it would be contrary to reporting standards for him to state that unaudited financial statements have been prepared in accordance with generally accepted accounting principles.

The addition of the suggested language would therefore be contrary to the spirit of Opinion No. 15.

Signing client's checks

Q. A client wishes to empower his accountant to sign checks during his absence of two weeks. The records and accounts would be kept by the company's employees. Would this procedure jeopardize the member's independence as auditor?

A. An alternative procedure was suggested. One of the client's six employees could sign checks in his absence. The checkbook, however, would be in the accountant's custody, the checks to be written under his scrutiny. The proprietor would review all transactions on his return.

Auditor as depositor
Financial interest, indirect

Q. A member, whose net worth is $10,000, has two accounts totaling $1,500 in a savings and loan association audited by his firm. Would this situation be considered to impair his firm's independence?

A. Deposits by a firm or by a partner or employee of a firm in a commercial bank or savings and loan association are not considered to constitute a direct financial interest in such bank or association. The deposits are considered to be an indirect interest, however, and if material, either in relation to the total assets of the bank or to the net worth of the auditor or his firm, the auditor's independence would be impaired.

In this case the deposits were not such as to impair the independence of the firm. However, another partner should be placed in charge of the audit of the savings and loan association. Moreover, if deposits in the association entitle the depositor to vote at the annual meeting, this right should not be exercised.

Financial interest, indirect
Family relationship

Q. The brother of an accounting firm's senior partner is the treasurer and a 26% stockholder of a client of the firm. Is the firm considered to be lacking in independence?

A. The firm is lacking in independence on two counts: (1) A reasonable observer who knew that the firm's senior partner was the brother of the client's treasurer would not be expected to consider the firm's opinion on the statements of such client to be independent, objective and unbiased; and (2) the accounting firm is considered to have a "material indirect financial interest" in the enterprise in question.

Financial interest, indirect
Family relationship

Q. When a client of a member sold stock for the first time to the public, the member purchased a thousand shares as an educational fund for his minor son. These holdings are not material in relation to the company's capitalization or to the auditor's net worth, but they are in relation to the son's personal fortune.

The member now will be required to express an independent opinion on the financial statements of the company. Does this situation involve a violation of Rule 1.01?

A. Transferring the financial interest to his son does not make the auditor's interest indirect. Consequently materiality is not a factor in assessing independence. This means that the auditor must either dispose of the financial interest or disclaim an opinion because of his lack of independence.

Financial interest, indirect

Q. Does ownership of stock in a Small Business Investment Company represent an indirect financial interest in the enterprises which borrow funds from the SBIC? Is ownership of shares in a mutual investment fund considered to be an indirect financial interest in the enterprises whose stock is held by the fund?

A. In both cases a member's financial interest would be considered "indirect" under Rule 1.01, and consequently the member's independence as auditor of such clients would not be jeopardized, unless the financial interest is material in relation to the client's total assets or to the member's own personal fortune.

Auditor as insurance policy holder
Financial interest, indirect

Q. A CPA auditing a mutual insurance company is a premium-paying policyholder and, by definition, a member of the company. May he, under Rule 1.01, express an independent opinion on the financial statements of the company?

A. As a policyholder the auditor is considered to have an indirect financial interest in the company. For this reason the test of materiality should be applied. If the premiums invested are not material either in relation to the total assets of the insurance company or to the net worth of the auditor or his firm, and if the auditor refrained from any voting privileges he might have, he would not be considered to be lacking in independence under Rule 1.01.

Auditor as landlord
Financial interest, indirect

Q. If a CPA owns or controls real estate rented by a client, would he be prohibited from rendering an opinion on that client's statements?

A. In general, it would not be desirable for a member to audit a client who rents property owned by the member, unless the rental or business value of such property to both the client and the CPA was so small as to be inconsequential

Financial interest, indirect

Q. If a CPA owns stock in a bank, may he audit a common trust fund operated by the trust department of that bank?

A. Ownership of stock in a bank would constitute an indirect financial interest in a common trust fund operated by the bank. Therefore, if the auditor's financial interest is material either in relation to the bank's total assets or to the auditor's personal fortune, he would not be considered independent in expressing an opinion on the financial statements of the common trust fund.

However, even though the auditor's financial interest in the bank may be immaterial, a third party having knowledge of all the facts may have some doubt as to the auditor's independence. For this reason, the auditor should divest himself of any financial interest in the bank prior to expressing an opinion on the financial statements of the common trust.

Financial interest

Q. Would the auditor of a parent company be considered independent if he was also a stockholder in a subsidiary of the company?

A. As a stockholder of the subsidiary company, the CPA would be interested in the financial well-being of the parent company, and consequently would not be considered independent. The committee regarded such a holding as a direct financial interest so that materiality would not be a factor.

The committee's opinion would be the same if the auditor of the subsidiary company was a stockholder in the parent company.

Financial interest

Q. A member has a substantial interest in a company which is indebted to a real estate corporation for an amount equal to less than 4% of the assets of the real estate company. He has been asked to assist another accounting firm in the auditing of the creditor corporation to which his company is in debt.

Would acceptance of the engagement involve a violation of Rule 1.01?

A. Since the financial interest in the client is indirect and apparently not material, acceptance of the engagement may not necessarily constitute a clear violation of Rule 1.01. Nevertheless, the relationship should be discouraged since a conflict-of-interest situation might arise in the future. There would be no objection to the member's assisting in the audit of the real estate corporation, provided the other accounting firm had responsibility for the audit and signed the opinion.

Financial interest

Q. May a CPA audit a country club of which he is a member, when membership involves the acquisition of one share of stock in the club?

A. Such stock ownership is not considered to be a financial interest in the club within the meaning of the independence rule. However, the auditor should not take part in the management of the club and should have nonmembers of the club within his firm perform the audit work. The auditor's membership in the club should be disclosed in his report.

Partnerships

Association of accountants not partners

Q. A member firm is considering a proposal from another partnership to practice jointly as associates, rather than as partners. It is planned that the staffs of the two firms be combined when necessary on large jobs. Each firm's name would appear on the letterhead of the other in small type as "Associates." In almost every other respect the two practices would be separate — that is, there would be separate names, billing, bookkeeping, etc.

A. The use of the term "Associates" has been considered misleading to the public if a partnership does not exist. A number of difficulties have arisen from affiliations of the type proposed. In general, members have been advised to form a partnership and have a written partnership agreement which would attempt to provide for most future contingencies and which would leave no one in doubt as to where responsibility lay for accounting work performed.

Association of accountants not partners

Q. Two CPAs, not partners, share an office, have the same employees, have a joint bank account and work together on each other's jobs. It is asked whether it would be proper to have a joint letterhead showing both names and "Certified Public Accountants" and address.

A. In these circumstances the public would assume that a partnership existed. If any reports were to be issued under the joint heading, it would be a violation of Rule 4.02.

Members should avoid the use of a letterhead showing the names of two accountants in such a way as to imply the existence of a partnership, when in fact a partnership does not exist.

Association of firms

Q. Three CPA firms wished to form an association to be known as "Smith, Jones & Associates." Is there any impropriety in this?

A. The committee looked with disfavor on the use of such a title, since it might mislead the public into thinking a true partnership existed. Instead, each firm was advised to use its own name on its letterhead, indicating the other two as correspondents.

Partner in two firms

Q. Is it unethical for a CPA to be a partner in two accounting firms?

A. Although nothing in the Code would prohibit a member from being a partner in two separate public accounting firms, such arrangements are discouraged for the following reasons:

1. It would be easy for the two different accounting firms to be on opposite sides of an issue arising between clients of the respective firms. A conflict of interest would clearly exist, at least in the mind of the partner of both firms.

2. The fact that the individual would be in a position to violate confidences might create suspicion in the minds of the clients of the two firms.

3. When new clients were referred to the joint partner he would have to decide which partnership was to receive the benefits. This might create unsatisfactory personal relationships.

Dual partnerships

Q. John Doe and Thomas Brown wish to form two partnerships, one in the former's city, to be known as John Doe and Company, and the other in the latter's city, to be known as Thomas Brown & Company. Is there any objection to this plan?

A. It might be desirable to have both names in the partnership title. That is, one firm might be known as Doe and Brown in Doe's city and the other as Brown and Doe in Brown's city.

Partner in individual practice

Q. May a CPA be a member of a firm of public accountants, all other members of which are noncertified, and at the same time retain for himself a practice on his own account as a CPA?

A. There would be no violation of the Code in such a situation. However, clients and others interested should be advised as to the dual position of the CPA to prevent any misunderstanding or misrepresentation.

Responsibility for non-CPA partner

Q. Is a CPA who has formed a partnership with a noncertified public accountant ethically responsible for all the acts of the partnership?

A. Yes. If the noncertified partner should violate the Institute's Code of Professional Ethics, the CPA would be held accountable.

Mixed partnerships
Signing reports

Q. May a CPA who is in partnership with non-CPAs sign reports with the firm name and below it affix his own signature with the designation "Certified Public Accountant"?

A. This would not be a violation of the Code, provided it is clear that the partnership itself is not being held out as composed entirely of CPAs.

Titles, partnership

Q. Is there any barrier in the Code of Professional Ethics to the use of an established firm name in a different state where there is some difference in the roster of partners?

A. No.

Titles, partnership

Q. A member asks if his firm may practice under a fictitious name which did not include the name of any individual. An illustration of such a partnership designation is "Northern Associates," followed by the CPA title. The member contends that such a designation is sometimes desirable. For example, when two or more small firms wish to merge, the use of the names of all partners might result in an excessively long title. Inability to agree on which names should be used and which dropped has prevented many desirable mergers. The member stated further that he has succeeded in registering the partnership title in question with his state board of accountancy.

A. The title of a CPA firm should consist of the names of one or more present or former partners. Impersonal and fictitious titles are misleading and might endanger the personal element in a relationship between professional accountants and their clients. It is in the best interests of the profession and the public to continue the traditional use of firm titles which denote a personal association and emphasize the personal responsibility and liability of the partners.

It was pointed out that the rules of conduct of professional societies, and the interpretations thereof, are often more restrictive than those of state accountancy boards. When such a difference exists the member is, of course, obliged to abide by the more restrictive ruling.

Titles, AICPA members

Q. May a firm, all of whose principals are Institute members, properly use the designation "Members of the American Institute of Certified Public Accountants," even though the firm title contains the name of a nonmember CPA who has withdrawn from the partnership and established another public accounting firm in the same area?

A. Yes.

Limited partners

Q. May a firm show on its letterhead as "limited" partners the names of persons formerly connected with the firm?

A. The listing was disapproved on the ground that such a practice may lead others to believe the limited partners are liable as active partners. Even if state law permits limited partnerships, the committee thought it would not be proper for a member firm to avail itself of this privilege.

Limited partner

Q. Would there be any violation of the Code if a member became a limited partner of his present firm?

A. It might be possible to work out such an arrangement legally, but the public could hardly be expected to inquire into the details of such a partnership arrangement to determine the relative liability of the individual partners with respect to the opinions rendered by the firm. It would be better for the partner to sever his connections with the firm and make some arrangement to render consulting services on a fee basis.

Retired partners
Letterheads
Directory listings

Q. The senior partner of an accounting firm after his retirement will continue to share in the net income of the firm for five years. Though he will be available for consultation, he will not be actively engaged in practice during his retirement. The following questions are asked: (1) How may his name be shown on the firm's letterhead? (2) How should his title and firm affiliation be indicated in the American Institute's membership directory? (3) Even though he will not occupy permanent office space with the firm after his retirement, may his name be listed in the yellow pages of the telephone directory?

A. (1) It is entirely proper for a firm to list on its letterhead the names of deceased or retired partners followed by their years of service. The names of retired partners usually appear at the beginning of the roster of partners followed by a line to distinguish them from the active partners. (2) It is common practice for retired partners to be listed as partners of the firm in the Institute's membership directory, if they so desire. (3) If a retired partner has office space or otherwise remains active with the firm, his association with the partnership may be shown in a building directory and in the white pages of the telephone directory. However, he should not have a listing in the yellow pages.

Solicitation

Other public accountants

Q. May a member use his firm letterhead for soliciting charitable contributions from other public accountants?

A. There is no objection to this practice, provided that such letters are sent only to other accountants in public practice. The member has a responsibility to see to it that his letter receives no other distribution, even when he supplies his firm letterhead to the charitable organization for printing and mailing.

Other public accountants

Q. A member plans to limit his practice to systems installation and analysis, accepting no auditing or tax work. May he write a letter to other public accounting firms announcing the opening of his office and offering his services through the firms to their clients?

A. There is no objection to this plan, provided that the mailing goes only to those engaged in public practice. Such a letter should not be sent to all CPAs, since many would be serving as controllers or treasurers of corporations served by other public accountants.

Other public accountants
Encroachment

Q. May a member write accountants and lawyers of his acquaintance announcing his availability as a tax consultant?

A. Since such a letter is not addressed to prospective clients, there would be no violation of the solicitation rule, nor would there be any encroachment on the practice of other public accountants, in violation of Rule 5.01. There was therefore no objection to the proposal.

Other public accountants
Tax chart

Q. A member has developed a chart for quickly figuring self-employment tax, which he would like to circularize among other accountants. He would use his own letterhead showing him to be a CPA and a member of the American Institute.

A. There is no objection to the proposed mailing of the chart. However, this circularization should be limited to practicing public accountants and should not be used as a means of soliciting clients.

Tax rulings, mailing of

Q. A CPA, a member of a social club, and formerly its auditor, became a member of the board of governors after another CPA member had been elected auditor.

Several weeks after this, he mailed a copy of an income tax ruling which offered advantages to the club, together with his own comments, on his firm stationery, to all members of the board of governors. Is this a violation of the rules of conduct?

A. A member of a club has a right to inform the proper authorities regarding income tax rulings affecting the club. Although the more usual procedure would be to bring the matter to the attention of the president or the treasurer and to suggest that it be placed on the agenda for the next meeting of the board, there was no violation of the Code.

Estate planning
Letterheads

Q. A member has rendered accounting services in connection with estate planning, together with an attorney and two insurance underwriters — each billing and being paid separately for his services. The underwriters wish to prepare a letterhead for estate practice use and for solicitation of clients. They have suggested, since legal and accounting services are recognized as a necessary adjunct to this type of practice, that the attorney's and the CPA's names be displayed on the letterhead, with titles. Would this violate the Code of Professional Ethics?

A. The suggested letterhead, which would be used in soliciting and promoting business, would place the CPA in violation of ethics committee Opinion No. 2, which holds that a member may not carry out through others acts which he is prohibited from performing directly.

There is nothing in the Code of Professional Ethics to prevent a member from collaborating with insurance underwriters and attorneys in the estate planning field, but since such services are of a type performed by public accountants, a member must observe the by-laws and the Code of Professional Ethics in rendering these special services.

Offer of gratis service
Encroachment

Q. May a member offer in a church bulletin to prepare without charge Federal and state income tax returns of all persons agreeing to contribute to the church's emergency fund?

A. Such an offer would be an attempt to obtain clients by solicitation and consequently would be a violation of Rule 3.02. The offer would also be a violation of Rule 5.01, forbidding encroachment upon the practice of another public accountant.

Change of control of client company

Q. A member states that control of a client company has been obtained by a second company which is served by another accounting firm. Would there be any violation of Rule 3.02 if the member communicated with the holding company and the accounting firm in an effort to retain his client?

A. No. He would be free to do so because of the existing client relationship.

Partnership, withdrawal from
Clients of former partnership

Q. A member has withdrawn from a partnership and is entering a new partnership. The partnership agreement in his former firm was oral and contained no provisions for division of clients. May the member send annnouncements to the clients he served in the former partnership?

A. Yes.

Clients of dissolved partnership

Q. In the absence of any arrangement on the point, may a former partner of a firm now dissolved solicit for his own account the former clients of the partnership?

A. Yes. The goodwill of a partnership is the goodwill of all the partners, and, unless otherwise agreed, the clients of such a firm are the clients of all the partners.

An equitable arrangement is one under which all former partners write a joint letter to all former clients requesting such clients to indicate their wishes as to which of the former partners should carry out the assignment and retain the working papers. After such an indication by the client any solicitation of that client by another former partner would be cause for discipline under the Institute's Code of Professional Ethics.

Feasibility study

Q. An accounting firm has been approached by a prospective client. Does the firm's offer for members of its staff to spend two or three days on the potential client's records without charge, collecting facts for the purpose of making a feasibility study, represent a violation of professional ethics?

A. Nothing in the Institute's Code of Professional Ethics requires the accounting firm to charge for the service rendered.

Indirect solicitation
Fee sharing

Q. A CPA firm wishes to enter into an agreement with a management specialist who is communicating with local business organizations. He would prepare a survey of the business for the purpose of bringing to light suggested areas of improvement. If the survey indicated deficiencies in the accounting system, then the CPA firm would be contacted as professional men well qualified to design and install accounting systems.

Compensation to the management specialist would be paid by the CPA and would be based upon a percentage of the total fee for the engagement.

A. There is nothing wrong in a member's accepting referrals. Nearly all CPAs have benefited by having their names suggested to prospective clients by bankers and businessmen. In these cases, however, the referral springs from goodwill and not from the expectation of a fee.

But when a management services specialist communicates with business organizations to survey their corporate structures for systems improvement, and engages a CPA firm to do all the accounting work which he uncovers from this source, then the CPA firm would not be complying with Opinion No. 2. This procedure does not come within the area of permissible referrals, because the management services specialist would be functioning, in a sense, as an agent for the CPA.

The proposal would also violate Rule 3.04, which prohibits the sharing of professional fees with nonpractitioners.

Indirect solicitation
Trade associations

Q. May a member retained by a trade association permit the association to offer his services to its members?

A. This would be indirect solicitation in violation of Rule 3.02. It would also violate Opinion No. 2, which prohibits a member from carrying out through others acts which he may not do directly.

Indirect solicitation
Trade associations

Q. A CPA is employed by a trade association and is paid a fixed salary for taking charge of the retail bookkeeping service department. This department offers bookkeeping services to the individual members of the association who subscribe to the service. The association freely asks its members to subscribe to the service, without mention of the fact that the department is run by a CPA.

Has the CPA in question violated the prohibitions against advertising, solicitation, and encroachment?

A. The CPA in question would not necessarily be violating the Institute's Code of Professional Ethics if he is merely an employee of the association, maintains no public accounting practice, is not held out as a public accountant, and does not violate the state accountancy law.

Indirect solicitation
Trade associations

Q. May a member send letters to trade associations offering to speak at their meetings on subjects of general interest on which he is well informed?

A. Addresses by accountants before business groups are highly desirable, but it is preferable that such addresses be delivered in response to unsolicited invitations or through arrangement by state or national professional organizations of accountants. Direct solicitation of opportunities to speak before trade associations might be regarded as violations of the prohibitions against advertising, solicitation and encroachment.

Trade associations
Industry surveys

Q. An accounting firm would like to send out a questionnaire to a number of companies in the same industry. The transmittal letter, which would be signed by the firm's director of research, would not show any professional designation. The information gathered would be used both for the firm's clients and in the preparation of printed articles.

A. While the issuance of an industry-wide survey questionnaire may not directly violate the Code, it is preferable for such surveys to be carried out through trade associations rather than by an accounting firm.

Trade associations
Industry surveys

Q. An accounting firm accepted an engagement to conduct a survey and to compile statistics for a trade association. The letter sent out by the association referred to the accounting firm by name and requested that replies be sent to the firm. The questionnaire went to all members of the association, some of whom were undoubtedly served by other public accountants. Does this mailing violate the prohibitions against advertising and solicitation?

A. There is nothing improper in a firm's undertaking such an engagement. This is a legitimate professional service which CPAs are qualified to perform.

Also, there is no impropriety in disclosing the name of the firm performing this service in communications requesting information from the association members, nor is there anything unethical in requesting members of the association to respond directly to the accounting firm.

Technical Standards

Audit reports, blank stationery

Q. A firm of CPAs, engaged to keep books of account for a client, prepares and issues a financial report on blank stationery without any indication as to who prepared the report and without any opinion regarding the financial statements. Is this a violation of the Code of Professional Ethics?

A. The Institute has no specific rule of ethics which would require that a member have a disclaimer in financial reports that are issued on blank stationery. Rule 2.03 deals only with statements with which the member's *name is associated*. However, Statements on Auditing Procedure No. 33

says in effect that when no audit has been performed, any financial statements with which the member is *in any way associated* should be marked on each page as unaudited. The auditing procedure committee believes it preferable that a disclaimer accompany such statements.

Audit reports
Use of "we" by sole practitioners

Q. May a sole proprietor use the plural pronoun "we" in expressing his opinion on financial statements?

A. The use of "I" and "we" by a single practitioner is of little significance.

Testimony as expert witness
Tax fraud

Q. How far may a CPA go in testifying as an expert witness in tax fraud cases? When he gives testimony that is proved false, can he be charged, under Rule 1.02, with having committed an act discreditable to the profession?

A. A member should be permitted to testify as an expert witness as long as he is technically competent to do so. He must bear in mind, however, that he is being called upon to express an independent professional opinion and that he must therefore observe the required technical and ethical standards.

If it were shown that statements, schedules or testimony presented by him were misleading or contained material misstatements, he could be charged with a violation of Rule 1.02.

Confirmation procedure, performed by others

Q. May a member make use of an outside mailing service for the confirmation of receivables and payables? The service would mail requests for confirmation on behalf of accounting firms. The returned confirmations would be removed from the envelope and given to the public accounting firm.

A. The member would be in violation of Rule 2.01 if he subscribed to such a service, since he would be relying for an important feature of his examination upon the work of another upon whom he had no right to rely.

Confirmation procedure
Incompatible occupations, collection agent

Q. May a member send out confirmation notices for the purpose of collecting a client's accounts?

A. The use of confirmation notices should be restricted to their technical purposes, although there can be no criticism of the accountant if a legitimate notice to confirm accounts receivable happens to result in payment of an account. The use of accountants' confirmation notices for the sole purpose of collecting a client's accounts, and not in connection with an audit or examination, is improper.

Tax practice, error in previous year's return

Q. A corporation has engaged a CPA to prepare its current year's income tax return without audit. The corporation has prepared its own returns for the last two years. In examining the previous year's tax return, the member discovered an error which resulted in a substantial underpayment of tax. The error was brought to the attention of the officers of the corporation, with the recommendation that an amended return be filed. However, the officers said they were willing to take their chances that the error would not be discovered. May the member prepare and sign the current year's return?

A. The accountant fulfilled his duty when he notified the client of the error made in the previous year's return. There is therefore no reason why he may not prepare and sign the current return.

General

Auditor as employee

Q. A member has become an employee of a company with extensive outside interests. The employers desire the member to make audits of these corporate interests and render an opinion primarily for their own information. These reports would undoubtedly be available to the other stockholders. Would there be any violation if these examinations were made and signed by the member?

A. If the member has given up practice as a public accountant, he may properly perform any services required by his employer, including making an examination of the accounts of minority-owned companies. Nothing in the Code would prevent him from using his CPA title, although his status as an employee should be made clear in the reports.

Auditor engaged by attorney

Q. A CPA has been engaged by an attorney to do accounting work for an estate. The accountant prepared his report but instead of consulting with the attorney he submitted it directly to the administrator. Was this a violation?

A. While it would have been desirable for the accountant to notify the attorney of the completion of his report, there was no violation of professional ethics in the accountant's submitting the report to the administrator.

Auditor engaged by company president

Q. The president of a corporation, who owns 70% of the common stock, called in a CPA to audit the books for the purpose of using the financial statements to increase the mortgage on corporation property. The board of directors had not been advised, even informally, of the additional mortgage. Should the CPA have requested a letter from the president to perform the services, in which it would be stated that the matter had been approved by the board of directors?

A. There is no reason why a member, at the request of the president of a corporation, should not prepare financial statements for his company for any purpose. The CPA could assume that it is up to the president to clear with the board of directors and the stockholders and comply with any legal technicalities that might be necessary in connection with increasing the mortgage indebtedness.

Bookkeeping service as "feeder"
Confidential relationship

Q. A member contemplates opening an office and subletting space to a business service organization, offering bookkeeping, secretarial and telephone answering service.

1. If the bookkeeping service organization advertises and otherwise solicits customers, can any impropriety be imputed to the member because of the tenant-lessor arrangement?

2. In using the secretarial services of the organization for the typing of tax returns, audit reports and other client papers, would there be a violation of the confidential relationship between member and his clients?

A. The proposed plan, if not an actual violation of the rules, would come so close to being one that the member was advised not to proceed with it.

1. If the service company was housed in the same quarters, the general public would assume that there was only one operation. There was also the danger that the sub-tenant's activities would serve as a "feeder" to the member's practice.

2. The use of the secretarial service would violate the rule on confidential relationship.

Fees, collection of notes issued in payment of

Q. An accounting firm made arrangements with a bank to collect notes issued in payment of fees due, and so advised a client who was delinquent. The client questioned the ethics of this procedure.

A. The procedure followed does not violate any provision of the Code of Professional Ethics.

Illegal acts of client

Q. A member firm is acting as consultant for a corporation conducting a small loan business. The company makes loans to persons who purchase $30 worth of stock for each $100 face value of the loan. This practice appears to be in violation of the small loan act and could result in action against the directors, as well as revocation of their license to do business. May the firm continue to act as consultant for this corporation?

A. No rule of professional conduct would be violated if the firm continued in this capacity. However, it was felt that it might be wise for the firm to withdraw in order to avoid possible embarrassment by litigation.

Referrals by bank

Q. A member, unmarried and living with his parents, has an office in a building owned and occupied by a bank, of which his father is president. The father refers customers to the son for the preparation of financial statements used by the bank for credit purposes. Is this situation ethically sound?

A. There is no reason why the father should not favor the son, if he is a competent practitioner and does not violate the confidential relationship between himself and the recommended clients. The bank, however, cannot be one of the son's audit clients.

Tax practice
Conflict of interest

Q. An Institute member is in partnership with a non-CPA, who is a former internal revenue agent, with several years' experience as a practitioner specializing in taxes. Tax work accounts for approximately half of the firm's gross fees. The non-CPA has been asked to serve, without compensation, as the public member of the board of tax appeals recently established under a municipal income tax ordinance. Would his acceptance be advisable, provided he disqualified himself in any case in which he was directly or indirectly connected?

A. The position should be declined, since it would be difficult for the partnership to avoid conflicts of interest. However, if the firm did not handle municipal tax matters, there would be no conflict of interest, and the non-CPA could properly accept the position.

Index

INDEX

NOTE: Page numbers in italics refer to Appendices A-D, pages 175-302.

305